Backroad Bicycling
Near New York City

Backroad Bicycling Near New York City

GERRY BROOKS

25 One-Day Bike
Tours in Connecticut,
New York,
New Jersey, and
Pennsylvania

THE COUNTRYMAN PRESS
WOODSTOCK, VERMONT

AN INVITATION TO THE READER Although it is unlikely that the roads you cycle on these tours will change much with time, some road signs, landmarks, and other items may. If you find that such changes have occurred on these routes, please let the author and publisher know, so that corrections may be made in future editions. Other comments and suggestions are also welcome. Address all correspondence to: Editor, Backroad Bicycling Series, Backcountry Guides, P.O. Box 748, Woodstock, VT 05091.

Copyright © 2004 by Gerry Brooks
First Edition

LIBRARY OF CONGRESS CATALOGING-IN-PUBLICATION DATA
Brooks, Gerry
    Backroad bicycling near New York City : 25 one-day bike tours in
  Connecticut, New York, New Jersey, and Pennsylvania / Gerry Brooks.—
  1st ed.
        p. cm.
  ISBN 0-88150-660-5
  1. Bicycle touring—New York Region—Guidebooks. 2. New York Region—
  Guidebooks.
  I. Title
  GV1045.5.N3B76 2004
  796.6'4'09747—dc22   2004047759

Cover and interior design by Bodenweber Design
Composition by PerfecType, Nashville, TN
Cover photograph © Dennis Coello
Interior photographs by the author
Maps by Moore Creative Designs, © The Countryman Press

Published by The Countryman Press, P.O. Box 748, Woodstock, Vermont 05091

Distributed by W.W. Norton & Company, Inc., 500 Fifth Avenue, New York, NY 10110

Printed in the United States of America

10 9 8 7 6 5 4 3 2 1

To my wife, Arlene, who in her own special way was a constant source of creative energy, support, and encouragement.

To Arlene and my daughter, Gail, for their dedicated and professional leadership with Brooks Country Cycling Tours.

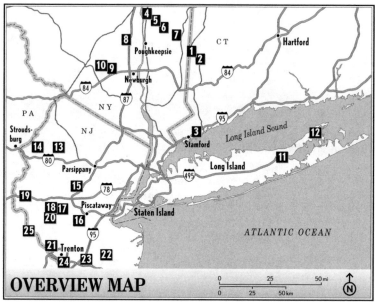

OVERVIEW MAP

0   25   50 mi
0   25   50 km

© The Countryman Press

CONTENTS

15 Introduction

CONNECTICUT

26 **1** Connecticut Countryside Day Trip
34 **2** Lake Waramaug/Metric Century
43 **3** Connecticut Shore to Redding

NEW YORK

55 **4** Rhinebeck Day Trip
61 **5** Clinton to Rhinebeck
69 **6** Millbrook to Clinton Corners
77 **7** Dutchess County, Northeast
84 **8** New Paltz to Rosendale
92 **9** New Paltz Day Trip
99 **10** Gunks, Ho!
106 **11** Long Island Berries and Wine
113 **12** Shelter Island

NEW JERSEY

124 **13** Andover to Hope
130 **14** New Jersey's Great Northwest
138 **15** Somerset County
147 **16** Canals and Bridges
153 **17** Deer Path to Oldwick
161 **18** Frenchtown Treasures
166 **19** The Delaware's Banks
175 **20** Flemington to Lumberville, Pennsylvania
181 **21** The Delaware's Paths and Trails
189 **22** Turkey Swamp to Allentown

195 **23** Allentown with a Twist
203 **24** Three Counties

PENNSYLVANIA
212 **25** Bucks County

ACKNOWLEDGMENTS My thanks to our many loyal clients who returned to cycle with us throughout the years. Their enthusiastic participation and support for our cycling program were essential in helping us to evolve and create our one-day touring program that is described in this tour guide.

BACKROAD BICYCLE TOURS AT A GLANCE

* = Tours reachable by train from New York City

RIDE	REGION	DISTANCE
1. Connecticut Countryside Day Trip	Connecticut	28/45 miles
2. Lake Waramaug/Metric Century	Connecticut	44/52/62.5 miles
3. * Connecticut Shore to Redding	Connecticut	25/45 miles
4. * Rhinebeck Day Trip	New York	31/42 miles
5. Clinton to Rhinebeck	New York	27/35/46 miles
6. Millbrook to Clinton Corners	New York	31/39/48 miles
7. * Dutchess County, Northeast	New York	40/50 miles
8. New Paltz to Rosendale	New York	30/43 miles
9. New Paltz Day Trip	New York	44 miles
10. Gunks, Ho!	New York	26/42/52 miles
11. * Long Island Berries and Wine	New York	36/40 miles
12. * Shelter Island	New York	27/42/60 miles
13. Andover to Hope	New Jersey	40/46 miles

DIFFICULTY	BIKE	HIGHLIGHTS
Moderate	Road	Kent Village, Bull's Covered Bridge, Webatuck Crafts Village
More Difficult	Road	Kent Village, Lake Waramaug State Park, Hopkins Vineyards, New Preston antiquing, Bull's Covered Bridge, Webatuck Crafts Village
Easy to Moderate	Road	Long Island Sound views, Campo Beach in Westport
Moderate	Road	Rhinebeck Village, Clermont State Park
Moderate	Road	Rhinebeck Village; ride accessible by train
Moderate	Road	Institute of Ecosystem Studies, Millbrook Village, Millbrook Vineyards
Moderate	Road	Harlem Valley Rail Trail, Millerton Village
Moderate to More Difficult	Hybrid	New Paltz Village, Rosendale, Wallkill Valley Rail Trail
Easy to Moderate	Hybrid	New Paltz Village, Wallkill Valley Rail Trail, Rivendell Winery, the Shawangunk Ridge (the Gunks)
Moderate	Road	The Shawangunk Ridge (the Gunks)
Easy	Road	Gallucio Family Winery, Wickham's Fruit and Vegetable Farm, New Suffolk Beach
Easy to Moderate	Road	Ram's Head Island, Crescent Beach, town of Greenport, town of Sag Harbor
Moderate	Road	Hope Village, Andover Village, Kittatinny State Park

RIDE	REGION	DISTANCE
14. New Jersey's Great Northwest	New Jersey	44/51 miles
15. * Somerset County	New Jersey	37 miles
16. Canals and Bridges	New Jersey	24/37 miles
17. Deer Path to Oldwick	New Jersey	39/48 miles
18. Frenchtown Treasures	New Jersey	35 miles
19. The Delaware's Banks	New Jersey/ Pennsylvania	26/42 miles
20. Flemington to Lumberville, Pennsylvania	New Jersey/ Pennsylvania	30/38 miles
21. The Delaware's Paths and Trails	New Jersey/ Pennsylvania	33/40 miles
22. Turkey Swamp to Allentown	New Jersey	45 miles
23. Allentown with a Twist	New Jersey	41/50 miles
24. Three Counties	New Jersey	39/44 miles
25. Bucks County	New Jersey/ Pennsylvania	39 miles

DIFFICULTY	BIKE	HIGHLIGHTS
Moderate	Road/Hybrid	Blairstown Airport, Andover Village
Moderate	Road	Leonard J. Buck Gardens, Oldwick Village, Pottersville Historic District
Easy to Moderate	Hybrid	Colonial Park Gardens, Delaware and Raritan State Park Recreation Trail
Moderate to More Difficult	Road	Oldwick Village, Mountainville Village
Moderate	Road	Frenchtown Village, Uhlerstown Covered Bridge
Easy to Moderate	Road	Milford Village, Roebling-designed Riegelsville Bridge
Easy to Moderate	Road/Hybrid	Liberty Village at Flemington; Flemington Village; Prallsville Mill Site; Lumberville Village; Fleecy Dale Road; Carversville, Pennsylvania
Moderate	Hybrid	Washington Crossing State Park; Lumberville and New Hope, Pennsylvania; Lambertville, New Jersey; Delaware Canal Park Recreation Trail
Easy	Road	Turkey Swamp Park, Allentown Village
Easy	Road	Roosevelt and Crosswicks, Historic Walnford Village, Allentown Village
Easy	Road	Historic Walnford Village
Moderate to More Difficult	Road	Bucks County covered bridges, Lumberville, Carversville, Pearl S. Buck Home

INTRODUCTION   Although not all of the tours chosen for this guide follow flat terrain, the name *Cycling for Softies* could be given to this compilation of one-day trips in New York's tri-state area. Whether you choose to enjoy riding solo, with friends, or as a family, this guide gathers all the information that you might need to make your day fun. Just transport yourself and your bicycle to the starting point of the tour and savor a day of pleasant cycling in the countryside.

When we think about New York, very often the image that we conjure is that of a vast metropolitan environment with traffic sprawling for miles between New York City's main business districts and the many suburban bedroom communities that spread from them in all directions. If we take a closer look, however, we can discover many delightful quiet country roads and lanes within a drive of one hour and fifteen minutes to one hour and forty-five minutes from New York City.

On these networks of country lanes we find what are truly cyclists' delights. Fields open up before us, providing beautiful vistas of the countryside. Horse or dairy farms present picturesque images as we cycle by them. During the summer lakes welcome us as we stop and enjoy a swim and a picnic lunch. We might visit one of the many wineries along some of these routes and take part in a tour and a tasting. The Hudson Valley's wineries as well as the vineyards found at the east end of Long Island's North Fork are well regarded for having produced notable vintages. Or we might partake of seasonal fruit picking, or antiquing in some of the many small villages offering such an enjoyable interlude. All of these sights and activities take place on quiet country roads where there's light traffic volume.

Within each tour in this guide you'll find notes on distance and terrain, driving directions and driving times from New York City to the start of the tour, and detailed directions with suggested points of interest along the route. Some of the tours start at or near local train stations and can be reached by train. These are noted in the Driving Directions within the tours themselves. Also included are recommendations for where you may both purchase and enjoy eating your lunch and the locations of cycle shops in some areas should you need assistance or wish to shop. Also offered is what every cyclist needs: a cue sheet and map of each tour that will readily fit into your map carrier for easy viewing when you stop to look at your directions.

Small-town bakeries—this one in Milford, New Jersey—offers delicious snacks.

ABOUT THE RIDES Each tour is quite unique and is routed along roads that enable you to enjoy intimate contact with the countryside. It may be a good idea to reread the description of the day's tour before setting off on your ride each day in order to familiarize yourself with the route and any points that are of special interest.

The rides average between 35 and 45 miles in length (excluding optional loops) and are all rated according to the difficulty of the terrain. It is helpful to note that at a casual touring pace a cyclist will ride 8–10 miles per hour. Each tour is mapped out in a loop that brings you back to the point where you began the ride.

Optional loops of 6–12 miles that can extend some of the rides usually occur at lunchtime or at the end of the ride. This gives energetic riders an opportunity to add some additional miles while others can relax and enjoy eating a treat or perhaps doing some antiquing in a local village. It's also interesting to note that many of these rides are adjacent to one another. The overall map of the region including each of the rides in this guide (see page 6) makes it possible to plan a mini vacation of two or three days by combining several one-day tours.

All of these rides are suitable for kids over 12 years of age if they are fairly enthusiastic cyclists; there's low traffic volume on every route, and mileage can be kept to a minimum by eliminating the optional rides on the tours that have them.

The cue sheets for the tours have been written in a clear and concise format. Having a cyclometer on your bicycle will give you a more exact measurement of the mileage between turns. There still might be some slight discrepancies in mileage, however, because individual cyclometers may be calibrated somewhat differently.

Also worth noting is that actual signposting may vary at times from that indicated on a cue sheet; signs may be missing or, though it occurs less frequently, a road name may be changed. If you come across any of these discrepancies on your way, very often consulting the map will eliminate any confusion. It is helpful to have a street-level road map in your bag to consult if you stray off course.

TOUR RATINGS   People often view differently the level of difficulty of cycling terrain. As an example, we once had a client who
joined us on a tour that was rated easy. The ride was almost flat
throughout its 25-mile route. We did, however, have to cycle on an
overpass over a major artery, at which point the client stated, "I
thought you said the route was easy!"

I've tried to give you an accurate picture of the terrain of each
ride by using the following ratings.

Easy Terrain

Characterized by a flat to gently rolling landscape. There may be
one or two places where the terrain rolls more steeply, but the
steeper climbs are short. These tours are suitable for three-speed
bicycles.

Moderate Terrain

Characterized by a combination of easy and more rolling terrain.
For the most part any climbs, while they may be steep, are also
short in distance. There may be one or two longer climbs, with
each usually not exceeding $\frac{1}{4}$ mile.

More Difficult Terrain

Characterized by a combination of easy, rolling terrain throughout
and one or two more difficult climbs, each of which usually does
not exceed a mile in distance.

PREPARING FOR A TOUR   For those who've never ridden 35–40
miles, these numbers may sound intimidating. With a little prepa-
ration, however, anyone who is healthy can both ride this distance
and enjoy all the benefits that come with spending a day outdoors
on a bicycle in the country. Riding at a leisurely touring pace of
8–10 miles per hour and allowing for stops along the way means
that a 35–40 mile ride should take about five to five and a half
hours. It may be helpful to think of the distance to be covered in a
ride in terms of hours rather than miles. If you're planning your
first ride, you may want to select one that's rated as easy and
then work your way up to rides that are moderate.

A rearview mirror mounted on your helmet can be a big help as you ride.

The best method of getting into shape for recreational bicycle touring is to get on a bicycle and pedal two or three times per week. If you have an indoor bicycle trainer and pedal for 30 minutes a few times each week, you'll notice that your stamina builds quickly. Your speed, pedaling cadence, and distance will increase in a short period of time.

Before beginning any tour, make sure that your bicycle is in good repair and is inspected by a reputable local bike shop if it's been two years or more since its last tune-up. Later on in this introduction I'll give you suggestions on what to look for when checking your bicycle for safe operation.

Plan on wearing clothing that breathes, insulates, and wicks moisture away from your skin so that you feel comfortable and dry. Wool and polypropylene are the favored choices of today's cyclists. Remember that as you ride you'll want to keep your muscles warm, especially those in your legs. Wear layers that cover your thighs and knees so that as you warm up, you can peel them off.

WHAT TO BRING ON A ONE-DAY TOUR   Following is a list of accessories that will make your riding safe and more enjoyable and will help you to deal with any extenuating circumstances that arise on your trip.

- Map clip or front handlebar bag with a map carrier. This will keep route directions and maps readily visible and available to you. If you don't have a map holder, you can improvise by using clothespins or stationary clips to attach the directions to the cable housing above the handlebars. You may also wish to carry some personal accessories in a front handlebar bag. Note that it's not advisable to put too much weight in a front bag; this could destabilize your front wheel and throw off your balance. It's best to keep more weight behind you, on either a rear rack or in a seat or wedge bag.

- Water bottle. Water is your main source of fuel; you should remember to drink before you're thirsty, preferably every time you stop for a rest. If it's a warm day, it may be wise to carry two water bottles on your bike.

- Snacking food. Carrying some snacking food with you and nibbling on it periodically will help to keep up your energy level. Wise snacking choices include fruits such as apples, bananas, and oranges. Nuts and raisins also provide an energy boost because they're high in complex carbohydrates.

- Set of tire irons, spare tube, and frame pump. Nine times out of 10 an on-the-road mechanical problem is a tube puncture. Learn how to fix a flat and have available the tools and spare tube needed to make this repair.

- Basic first-aid kit. Having it will help you to deal with any scraped elbows and knees in case of a spill.

- Sunglasses, sunblock, padded cycling gloves. All of these contribute to your comfort and safety as you ride.

- Thin, waterproof nylon shell or jacket. This will keep you warm in the event that the weather turns cool or windy, and dry in the event of a sudden rain shower. Make sure this and all your clothing is brightly colored, which makes you more visible to drivers.

- Lightweight security cable. This will deter anyone from taking your bike should you decide to stop for an indoor lunch.

- Rearview mirror. This can be mounted either on the bicycle's handlebars, your helmet, or your glasses. When you come to an obstacle in the road, the mirror will enable you to determine quickly, without having to turn around, whether it's safe to avoid it by swerving into the road from the shoulder. Keeping your attention focused forward will also allow you to see the beauty of the countryside, which will make the riding more enjoyable.

- Helmet. This is the most important item to have with you. Today's helmets are lightweight with plenty of ventilation channels that will keep you cooler in the summer and warmer on cool days. Always wear a helmet when riding!

SAFETY ON THE ROAD   Here I take time for a brief but important list of safe riding habits and practices that can reduce your chances of having an accident on the road.

- Ride in single file on the right side of the road with the flow of traffic.

- Keep at least three bike lengths between you and the cyclist in front of you to insure safe stopping for yourself should the cyclist in front of you stop.

- Always pull your bicycle off the paved road surface when stopping to allow both cars and other cyclists to pass you.

- When passing another cyclist, always do so on the left, always tell him or her that you are passing, and always return immediately to your lane on the right.

- Obey all traffic control devices, which include traffic lights, stop signs, and yield signs.

- Always signal your intention to turn or stop by extending your left hand and arm straight out for a left turn; bending your left arm at the elbow and pointing up, palm facing forward, for a right turn; or pointing your left arm and hand downward, bent at the elbow with palm facing behind you, for stop. Those behind or in front of you, whether on bicycles or in cars, won't have to guess at your plans.

- Always dismount and walk across the road when making a left turn. Remember, you are crossing two lanes, which makes it more difficult to judge the speed of oncoming traffic.

- Pay attention to the road in front of you. If you see any road hazard that seems unsafe to ride over, such as sand, potholes, open sewer grates, and so forth, dismount and walk until you feel it's safe to get back on your bicycle and continue riding. Always dismount and walk across railroad tracks; you could have a serious fall if your wheels get caught in the tracks.

- When riding uphill, try to keep pressure off your pedals by downshifting to an easier gear in advance of the climb.

- When descending a hill, feather both front and rear brakes gently to control your speed. Bicycle brakes are very efficient today, and gentle tapping on your brakes will allow you to descend at a comfortable and safe speed. Always use both brakes when slowing or stopping your bicycle. Allow the cyclist in front of you to get down the hill before you descend. Never pass another cyclist on a downhill run. Should any water get onto your brake pads as you descend, the gentle feathering of your brakes will allow the friction to dry the brake pads and restore full and efficient braking.

A TWO-MINUTE BIKE SAFETY CHECK   At home before beginning your ride and again just before you set off for the day should you have transported your bicycle, it's wise to carry out a two-minute bicycle inspection to insure that your bicycle is in safe operating condition. If you find problems when performing this inspection, it may be wise to bring your bike into your local bicycle dealer or repair shop for a tune-up.

1. Squeeze the front wheel between your knees and try turning the handlebars. Grasp the saddle with both hands and twist it

from side to side and up and down. Neither the handlebars nor the saddle should turn.

2. Pick up the front wheel and spin it forward. The wheel should spin freely without any grinding sound. It should not wobble and touch the brake pads. Do the same with the rear wheel.

3. Check the tire pressure by grasping the metal wheel rim with four fingers and placing your thumb on the tire. Press down on the tire with your thumb. The tire should be firm; you should not be able to press your thumb into it. Tires should be inflated to their recommended PSI (pounds per square inch), which will be indicated on the sidewall of the tire. This will minimize the possibility of punctures and also make your riding more efficient.

4. Squeeze both brake levers gently until you feel them contact the wheel rims. There should be at least a $\frac{3}{4}$-inch distance between the brake levers and the handlebars. The levers should also return to their original position in a smooth action when they're released.

5. Check the quick release levers that hold the front and rear wheel onto the bicycle frame. They should not wobble when you apply some pressure to them, and they should point toward the bicycle.

6. Lift the bike about $\frac{1}{2}$ inch off the ground and drop it. If something has come loose, such as a water bottle holder or rear rack, you may be able to identify it by hearing the vibration of a loose screw.

FINAL THOUGHTS   The main objective of this guide is to introduce you to bicycle touring and all of its wonderful delights. There's a sense of peace and well-being created by the smooth action of your pedaling in a natural environment where nature is constantly revealing itself. As a family activity, the joys of cycling are hard to surpass. As a form of aerobics, cycling is a nonimpact exercise that provides a multiplicity of benefits for you both physically and mentally.

It's my hope that the suggestions made here will help prepare you and your family for many safe and fun-filled one-day cycling trips around New York's tri-state area. Because there may be changes on these routes over time, I always welcome your suggestions for updates. Cycle safely and enjoy!

CONNECTICUT

1

Connecticut Countryside Day Trip

- **TOUR DISTANCE:** 28 miles (45 miles with Option)
- **TERRAIN:** Moderate, with rolling terrain throughout. The rolling terrain on the Option has steeper grades.
- **SPECIAL FEATURES:** The village of Kent, Bull's Covered Bridge, Webatuck Village site

Litchfield County, Connecticut, is a pristine world of covered bridges and sugar maples, and three-hundred-year-old barns surrounded by meadows and stone walls. It's also rich in Colonial and Revolutionary War history.

Our ride starts in Sherman, Connecticut, named after Roger Sherman, a patriot and statesman and an original signer of both the Declaration of Independence and the U.S. Constitution. The quiet country lanes that lead to the town of Kent pass quite a few points of historical interest. Note the stump of the recently cut 250-year-old Washington Oak Tree on your right at mileage point 4.7 on the route. General Washington is said to have rested here. After taking you through Gaylordsville, the ride passes the Merwinsville Hotel, located beside the tracks of the old Housatonic Railway. This building is being restored and is now listed on the National Register of Historic Places. In the early 1840s Sylvanus Merwin discovered that a rail route was planned to go through Gaylordsville. After talking to surveyors and finding the exact location of the rail line, he purchased land on the east side of the Housatonic and erected a hotel in anticipation of the new business that the railroad would bring. When the representatives of the new rail line arrived to purchase the necessary rights-of-way, he refused to relinquish his property rights unless the railroads met his two demands: His hotel was to be used as a meal stop for all trains and the station was to be named after him. Because the railroad needed the land they agreed to his terms, and as a result the elegant Merwinsville Hotel opened its doors to the public in 1834 and remained in business for more than fifty years. Just beyond it on the right is the old Brown's Forge building.

Kent Village has one of those attractive main streets that can be found only in the old settled towns of New England. Interesting shops line the tree-lined thoroughfare. For lunch I recommend Stroble Bakery, which serves freshly made salads and desserts. Try a piece of the Skiff Mountain Pie for dessert! The Sloane Stanley Museum found at the far end of the village displays Eric Sloane's personal collection of early American tools. Sloane, a purveyor of Americana and author of books on traditional methods for doing just about everything around the house and farm in the pre-modern-day mid-Atlantic states, was best known for his paintings, murals, and illustrations.

A shorter return ride follows the western bank of the Housatonic River, while the longer Option loops out through the rolling terrain and farmland of Dutchess County, New York. After a rain, the water cascading down the overhangs of Schaghticoke Mountain provide a noticeable cooling of temperatures along the bicycle route here. The last few families of the Scatacook Indians, once the sole masters of this romantic region, still maintain a small reservation along this route. A short jog off the route leads to Bull's Covered Bridge, named for Jacob Bull. The bridge was completed in 1781 and was used to facilitate the transport of iron ore from New York State to a forge in Kent.

The optional loop rejoins the main tour just on the New York side of the border at Webatuck Crafts Village, a picturesque collection of 18th-century shops located beside the Ten Mile River. The Buttonwood Café, a favorite among bikers, makes for a delightful ice cream stop.

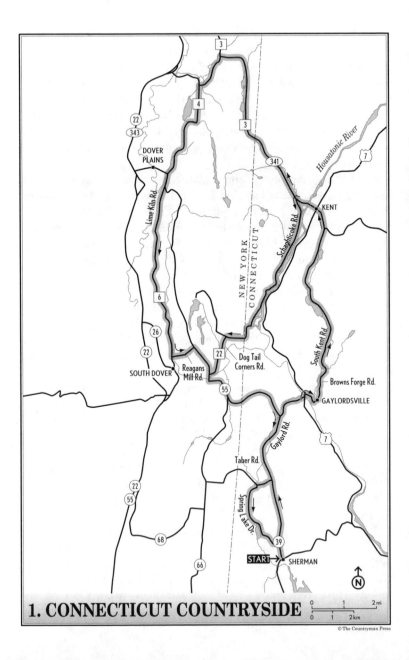

1. CONNECTICUT COUNTRYSIDE

0 1 2 mi
0 1 2 km

© The Countryman Press

0.0 Turn left from IGA parking area in Sherman onto CT 39
1.0 Turn right onto Church Road (becomes Gaylord Road)
4.7 Turn left onto US 7 (unmarked)
5.1 Make a hard right turn after bridge onto Station Road (unmarked)
5.2 Go straight on Station Road, passing South Kent Road
5.4 Continue on Station Road as it curves left
5.6 Continue straight onto Browns Forge Road
6.7 Turn right at the end of Browns Forge Road onto South Kent Road (unmarked)
11.0 Go straight onto CT 341
11.7 Turn right onto US 7/North Main Street to enter Kent, or continue on CT 341
12.5 Turn left onto Schaghticoke Road (unmarked); Option begins here
16.7 Turn right onto Dog Tail Corners Road (becomes CR 22) or turn left to
     Bull's Covered Bridge (0.4 mile)
17.7 Turn left at first crossroad (unmarked) to continue on Dog Tail Corners Road
19.1 Turn left at the end of Dog Tail Corners Road onto NY/CT 55 (unmarked)
22.1 Turn right onto CT 39
24.3 Turn right onto Taber Road
24.8 Turn left onto Spring Lake Drive
27.1 Turn right onto CT 39 (unmarked)
27.6 Turn right into IGA parking area on CT 39 to end tour

     Option (from mile 12.5)
0.0 Continue straight on CT 341 (becomes CR 3/Bog Hollow Road)
5.2 Turn left onto CR 4/Sinpatch Road
6.4 Turn left onto CR 4/Poplar Hill Road
9.4 Go straight onto Lime Kiln Road at Maple Avenue intersection
11.1 Turn left onto CR 6 (unmarked) after bridge
15.0 Turn left onto Reagans Mill Road
15.8 Bear right at the Y intersection and turn right immediately onto Berkshire Road
16.8 Bear right onto NY 22 (unmarked)
17.0 Continue at mile 19.1

DRIVING DIRECTIONS   Take the Henry Hudson Parkway north to the Saw Mill Parkway, and then the Saw Mill Parkway north to I-684 north. Continue straight on I-684 to the end where it becomes NY 22 north (do not take the exit for NY 22, which heads south). Continue straight on NY 22 north for approximately 6 miles and then turn right onto Haviland Hollow Road at the Putnam Diner, following the sign for CT 37. Turn left at the end of Haviland Hollow Road onto CT 37 toward Sherman. Merge left onto CT 39 in Sherman, then turn left at the gas station to continue on CT 39. Turn left immediately into the IGA Supermarket parking area and park in the rear.

On Saturday only there's a bathroom open in the town offices in the upper parking lot, and there's a bathroom inside the IGA Supermarket at the rear of the store.

Drive time from New York City is 1 hour and 30 minutes.

Whether cycling individually or in a group, you can enjoy the sun-dappled roads of the Connecticut countryside.

RIDE DIRECTIONS

0.0 Turn left from the Sherman IGA Supermarket parking area onto CT 39 north.

1.0 Turn right onto Church Road at the sign for the Sherman Congregational Church. Church Road becomes Gaylord Road.
Be careful on this road; it's bumpy with winding downhills. Just before the left turn onto CT 7 you'll pass the stump of the recently felled 250-year-old Washington Oak Tree.

4.7 Turn left at the end of Church Road onto unsigned US 7 north.

5.1 Make a hard right turn onto Station Road (unmarked) at Gaylordsville Country Store, just after crossing the bridge over the Housatonic River.

5.2 Go straight on Station Road, passing South Kent Road, and continue on Station Road as it curves left uphill.
After crossing the railroad tracks, the route passes the historic Merwinsville Hotel Train Station.

5.6 Continue straight onto Browns Forge Road.
Brown's Forge is on the right.

6.7 Turn right at the end of Browns Forge Road onto unmarked South Kent Road.

11.0 At the stop sign go straight onto CT 341 west toward Kent.

11.7 Turn right at the traffic light in Kent onto US 7 north/North Main Street.
Stroble Bakery is a good choice for lunch, although there are other choices on Main Street.

Leave Kent by reversing direction on US 7/Main Street, returning to the traffic light, and turning right onto CT 341 west.

12.5 Turn left onto Schaghticoke Road (unmarked).

The Option continues straight on CT 341 west.

16.7 Turn right at the end of Schaghticoke Road onto Dog Tail Corners Road, which becomes CR 22.
To visit Bull's Covered Bridge, turn left here and ride for 0.4 mile.

17.7 Turn left at the first crossroad you reach, at the house with the white picket fence, to continue on Dog Tail Corners Road.

19.1 Turn left at the end of Dog Tail Corners Road onto unmarked NY/CT 55.
Webatuck Crafts Village is on the right here, just beside the Ten Mile River. There are artisan's shops along with the Buttonwood Café, which makes for a timely ice cream stop.

22.1 Turn right onto CT 39 south toward Sherman.
The terrain here is rolling for 2 miles to the turn on Taber Road.

24.3 Turn right onto Taber Road.
The farm and countryside at the turn here are picture postcard perfect.

24.8 Take the first left onto Spring Lake Drive.
This is a spur road that rejoins CT 39, but it's well worth taking for its scenic beauty.

27.1 Turn right at the end of Spring Lake Road onto unmarked CT 39 south.

27.6 Turn right into the Sherman IGA Supermarket parking area to end the tour.

Option

0.0 From mile 12.5, continue straight on CT 341 west, passing Schaghticoke Road.
CT 341 west becomes CR 3/Bog Hollow Road. It crosses the Appalachian Trail 0.2 mile after passing Schaghticoke Road.

5.2 Turn left at the end of CT 341 onto CR 4/Sinpatch Road.

6.4 Turn left at the end of Sinpatch Road onto CR 4/Poplar Hill Road.
Located in the park on the left just before the turn is a monument to world peace. A rally for world peace is held here once a year.

9.4 Go straight onto Lime Kiln Road at the stop sign and intersection with Maple Avenue.

11.1 After the green bridge, turn left at the end of Lime Kiln Road onto unmarked CR 6.

15.0 Turn left onto Reagans Mill Road.
There's an uphill climb here.

15.8 Bear right at the Y intersection. At the end of Reagan's Mill Road turn right immediately onto Berkshire Road.
Be careful; there's a steep downhill just before the stop sign at CR 22.

16.8 Bear right onto unmarked CR 22.

17.0 Arrive at the Buttonwood Café.
Continue the tour from mile 19.1.

2

Lake Waramaug/Metric Century

- **TOUR DISTANCE:** 44 miles (52 miles with Option 1; 62.5 miles with Option 1 run twice)
- **TERRAIN:** More difficult, with hilly and rolling terrain throughout
- **SPECIAL FEATURES:** Kent Village, Lake Waramaug, Hopkins Winery, New Preston Village, Bull's Covered Bridge, Webatuck Village site

The Lake Waramaug and Metric Century day trips share the same route, but the Metric Century includes two additional loops that bring the cumulative trip mileage to 62.5. This tour takes place in Litchfield County, Connecticut, which is, as described in tour 1, Connecticut Countryside, a pristine world of covered bridges and sugar maples, and meadows bounded by centuries-old barns and stone walls.

Starting in Sherman, Connecticut, the route takes you past Gaylordsville and the historic Merwinsville Hotel to the village of Kent. (See page 26–27 in tour 1, Connecticut Countryside, for more detailed descriptions of these sights.) The route then veers to the east into the Litchfield Hills on the way to Lake Waramaug, the second largest natural lake in Connecticut, spanning 672 acres. At the lake you'll discover seasonal opportunities for swimming, picnicking, and canoeing at the state park. There's also an 8-mile cycling loop that meanders along the shoreline, passing attractive lakeside homes and offering pleasant views of the pastoral countryside. For more enthusiastic cyclists a second loop around the lake brings the total mileage at the conclusion of the ride to 62.5 miles, a metric century. At the far end of the lake there are opportunities for antiquing in the village of New Preston. A second enjoyable interlude consists of a stop at Hopkins Vineyards overlooking the lake. This is one of Connecticut's best-known wineries, with origins going back to 1787 when a Revolutionary War soldier named Elijah Hopkins claimed a homestead here. For years his family raised sheep and racehorses and grew grain and tobacco. The family entered the wine business in 1979 when they planted their first grapevines and converted their 19th-century barn into a state-of-the-art winery. A pleasant overnight or weekend can be spent at either the Inn at Lake Waramaug or the Boulders Inn, which are both located lakeside.

The route leaves the lake and continues in a westerly direction, passing through Bull's Covered Bridge. The bridge was completed in 1781 and was used to facilitate the transport of iron ore from New York State to a forge in Kent. On the New York State side of the border you can step back in time at the Webatuck Crafts Village, a picturesque collection of 18th-century shops where visitors can watch artisans throwing pots, blowing glass, and hammering metal into lamps. The Buttonwood Café's location beside the Ten Mile River offers the perfect place to relax and enjoy a well-earned ice cream cone.

DRIVING DIRECTIONS   Take the Henry Hudson Parkway north to the Saw Mill River Parkway, and then the Saw Mill River Parkway north to I-684 north. Continue straight on I-684 to NY 22 north (do not take the exit for NY 22, which heads south). Continue straight on NY 22 north for approximately 6 miles and turn right onto Haviland Hollow Road at the Putnam Diner, following signs for CT 37. Turn left at the end of Haviland Hollow Road onto CT 37 toward Sherman. Merge left onto CT 39 in Sherman, then turn left at the gas station to continue on CT 39. Turn left immediately into the IGA Supermarket parking lot and park in the rear of the lot.

On Saturday there is a bathroom open in the town offices in

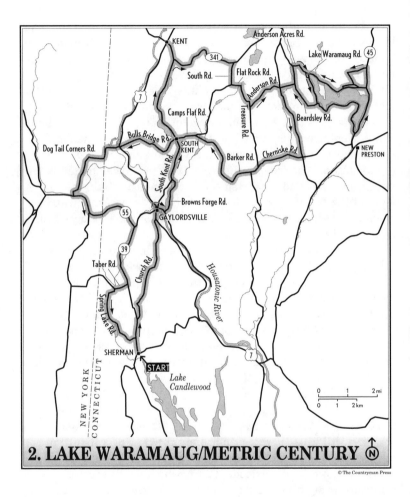

2. LAKE WARAMAUG/METRIC CENTURY

0.0	Turn left from IGA parking area in Sherman onto CT 39
1.0	Turn right onto Church Road
4.7	Turn left onto US 7 (unmarked)
5.1	Make a hard right turn after bridge onto Station Road (unmarked)
5.2	Go straight on Station Road, passing South Kent Road
5.4	Continue on Station Road as it curves left
5.6	Continue straight onto Brown's Forge Road
6.7	Turn right at the end of Brown's Forge Road onto South Kent Road (unmarked)
11.0	Go straight onto CT 341 west
11.7	Turn right onto US 7/North Main Street to enter Kent; turn left from US 7 onto CT 341 east to leave Kent
12.4	Continue on CT 341 at intersection with South Kent Road
14.9	Turn right onto South Road
15.6	Turn left onto Flat Rock Road
15.9	Turn right onto Treasure Road
16.7	Turn left onto Anderson Road (unmarked)
18.1	Bear left at Y intersection onto Kent Hollow Road
18.6	Turn left onto Beardsley Road
19.2	Bear right onto Anderson Acres Road
19.9	Bear right onto Lake Waramaug Road and continue to Lake Waramaug State Park picnic area
20.0	Leaving the picnic area with your back to the lake, turn left onto Lake Waramaug Road; Options 1 and 2 begin here
20.9	Turn right onto Golf Links Road
21.3	Turn right onto Beardsley Road
22.1	Turn left onto Kent Hollow Road
22.6	Turn left to continue on Kent Hollow Road (becomes Sawyer Hill Road)
25.1	Turn right onto Cherniske Road (unmarked) at intersection with New Preston Road on left
26.7	Continue straight on unmarked Barker Road (becomes West Meeting House Road) at intersection with Burnett Road
28.1	Go straight onto Camps Flat Road (unmarked)
30.6	Cross South Kent Road and go straight onto Bull's Bridge Road
32.9	Cross US 7 to continue on Bulls Bridge Road
33.3	Go straight onto CR 22/Dog Tail Corners Road
34.3	Turn left at first crossroads (unmarked) to continue on Dog Tail Corners Road
35.7	Turn left onto NY/CT 55 (unmarked)
38.7	Turn right onto CT 39 toward Sherman
40.9	Turn right onto Taber Road
41.4	Turn left onto Spring Lake Road
43.7	Turn right onto CT 39 (unmarked)
44.1	Turn right into IGA parking area on CT 39 to end tour

Option 1 (from mile 20.0)

0.0	Leaving the picnic area with your back to the lake, turn left onto Lake Waramaug Road
0.9	Bear left at the end of Lake Waramaug Road onto West Shore Road
3.7	Turn left at stop sign onto CT 45/East Shore Road
5.3	Turn left onto North Shore Road toward Hopkins Vineyard
5.6	Turn right onto Hopkins Road
5.8	Arrive at Hopkins Inn and Vineyard and continue straight onto Bliss Road
6.4	Turn right onto North Shore Road
7.6	Turn left onto Lake Waramaug Road
7.8	Arrive at Lake Waramaug State Park and continue from mile 20.0

Option 2 (from mile 20.0)

0.0	Leaving the picnic area with your back to the lake, turn left onto Lake Waramaug Road
0.9	Bear left at the end of Lake Waramaug Road onto West Shore Road
3.7	Turn left at stop sign onto CT 45/East Shore Road
6.0	Turn left onto Curtiss Road
6.7	Turn left onto Hopkins Road
7.2	Turn right onto Bliss Road
7.8	Turn right onto North Shore Road
9.0	Turn left onto Lake Waramaug Road
9.2	Arrive at Lake Waramaug State Park and continue from mile 20.0

the upper parking lot, and there is a bathroom inside the IGA Supermarket at the rear of the store.

Drive time from New York City is 1 hour and 30 minutes.

RIDE DIRECTIONS

0.0 Turn left from the IGA Supermarket parking area onto CT 39 north.

1.0 Turn right onto Church Road at the sign for the Sherman Congregational Church. Church Road becomes Gaylord Road.
Be careful on this road; it's bumpy, with winding downhills. Just before the left turn onto CT 7 you'll pass the stump of the recently felled 250-year-old Washington Oak Tree.

4.7 Turn left at the end of Church Road onto unmarked US 7 north.

5.1 Make a hard right turn onto Station Road (unmarked) at Gaylordsville Country Store, just after crossing the bridge over the Housatonic River.

5.2 Go straight on Station Road, passing South Kent Road, and continue on Station Road as it curves left uphill.
After crossing the railroad tracks, the route passes the historic Merwinsville Hotel Train Station.

5.6 Continue onto Browns Forge Road.
Brown's Forge is on the right.

6.7 Turn right at the end of Browns Forge Road onto unmarked South Kent Road.

11.0 At the stop sign go straight onto US 341 west toward Kent.

11.7 Turn right at the traffic light in Kent onto US 7 north/North Main Street.
Because there are no places between Kent and Lake Waramaug where you can purchase lunch, buying it in Kent and carrying it to the lake, where there's a nice picnic area, is worth considering. The Hopkins Inn at Lake Waramaug, opposite the Hopkins Winery, offers a full-service lunch on weekends.

Leave Kent by turning left onto CT 341 east at the traffic light.

12.4 Continue on CT 341 east toward Warren at the intersection with South Kent Road.
Be prepared for a steady, and at times steep, 2-mile climb here.

14.9 Turn right onto South Road.
The route still continues uphill.

15.6 Turn left onto Flat Rock Road.
Thank goodness it's over!

15.9 Take the first right onto Treasure Road.

16.7 Turn left onto unmarked Anderson Road.
Be careful on this steep, winding downhill.

18.1 Bear left at the Y intersection onto Kent Hollow Road.

18.6 Turn left at the end of Kent Hollow Road onto Beardsley Road.

Hopkins Winery is worth a stop.

19.2 Bear right at the Y intersection onto Anderson Acres Road.
There's a short but very steep climb here.

19.9 Bear right onto Lake Waramaug Road at the stop sign.

20.0 Arrive at Lake Waramaug State Park picnic area.
Here you'll find a pleasant picnic spot beside the lake. Swimming, bathrooms, and changing facilities are also available. Options 1 and 2 begin and end here.

To leave the picnic area, with your back to the lake, take a left onto Lake Waramaug Road.

20.9 Turn right onto Golf Links Road at the end of Lake Waramaug Road.
This part of the route is another short but steep climb.

21.3 Turn right at the end of Golf Links Road onto Beardsley Road.

22.1 Turn left onto Kent Hollow Road.
The terrain here continues to be rolling and traffic-free all the way to the Buttonwood Café.

22.6 Turn left to continue on Kent Hollow Road (which becomes Sawyer Hill Road).

25.1 Turn right onto unmarked Cherniske Road at the intersection with New Preston Road on the left.

26.7 Go straight onto unmarked Barker Road at the intersection with Burnett Road. Barker Road becomes West Meeting House Road.

28.1 Go straight onto unmarked Camps Flat Road.

30.6 Go straight across South Kent Road onto Bulls Bridge Road.

32.9 On Bulls Bridge Road cross US 7 at the traffic light and continue through Bulls Covered Bridge.

33.3 Go straight onto CR 22/Dog Tail Corners Road.

34.3 To continue on Dog Tail Corners Road, turn left at the first crossroads (unmarked) you reach, at the house with the white picket fence.

35.7 Turn left at the end of Dog Tail Corners Road onto unmarked NY/CT 55.
Webatuck Crafts Village is on the right here, just beside the Ten Mile River. You'll

find artisan's shops here along with the Buttonwood Café, which makes for a well-earned ice cream stop.

38.7 Turn right onto CT 39 south toward Sherman.

40.9 Turn right onto Taber Road.
The farm and countryside at this turn are picture postcard perfect.

41.4 Take the first left onto Spring Lake Road.
This is a spur road that rejoins CT 39, but its scenic beauty is worth seeing.

43.7 Turn right at the end of Spring Lake Road onto unmarked CT 39 south.

44.1 Turn right into the parking area of the Sherman IGA Supermarket to end the tour.

Option 1

0.0 From mile 20.0, leave the picnic area with your back to the lake and turn left onto Lake Waramaug Road.

0.9 Bear left at the end of Lake Waramaug Road onto West Shore Road.
This road is flat and quite picturesque, tracing the shoreline of the lake. Very attractive homes are situated on either side of the road.

3.7 At the stop sign turn left onto CT 45/East Shore Road.
The village of New Preston, with several interesting antiques shops, is located 0.4 mile to the right.

5.3 Turn left onto North Shore Road, toward Hopkins Vineyards.

5.6 Turn right onto Hopkins Road.
The road heads uphill to Hopkins Inn and Hopkins Vineyards.

5.8 Arrive at the Hopkins Inn on the right, and continue straight onto Bliss Road, returning to the lake.
Be careful; the road is a winding downhill here. To visit Hopkins Vineyards, turn right onto Hopkins Road. The winery is on the right roughly 50 yards from the turn.

6.4 Turn right at the end of Bliss Road onto North Shore Road.
The Inn at Lake Waramaug is just ahead.

7.6 Turn left onto Lake Waramaug Road.

7.8 Arrive at Lake Waramaug State Park.
Continue the tour from mile 20.0.

Option 2

0.0 From mile 20.0, leave the picnic area with your back to the lake and turn left onto Lake Waramaug Road.

0.9 Bear left onto West Shore Road at the end of Lake Waramaug Road.

3.7 Turn left at the stop sign onto CT 45/East Shore Road.

6.0 Turn left onto Curtiss Road.

6.7 Turn left onto Hopkins Road.
You'll pass Hopkins Vineyards on the left and the Hopkins Inn on the right.

7.2 Turn right onto Bliss Road.
Be careful here; the road twists downhill.

7.8 Turn right at the end of Bliss Road onto North Shore Road.

9.0 Turn left onto Lake Waramaug Road.

9.2 Arrive at Lake Waramaug State Park.
Continue the tour from mile 20.0.

3

Connecticut Shore to Redding

- **TOUR DISTANCE:** 25 miles (45 miles with Option)
- **TERRAIN:** Easy, with gentle terrain throughout. The Option is moderate, with rolling terrain throughout.
- **SPECIAL FEATURES:** Seasonal swimming, long water views of Long Island Sound

If you like the feeling of being near the sea, you'll enjoy this easy ride through Westport on shady roads lined with country estates. A good portion of this route traces the shoreline of Long Island Sound, treating us to panoramic views of the water, where there are swimming beaches and colorful sailing regattas are common during the summer.

Metro North's New Haven Line train from Grand Central Terminal stops at East Norwalk Station, just 0.8 mile from the start of the tour at Norwalk's Veterans Memorial Park.

The cycling leads through a very private and contemporary seaside subdivision of homes before continuing onto Greens Farms Road and Beachside Road. Mrs. Bolton's School for Girls, a prestigious private school that opened in 1926, was eventually renamed the Greens Farms Academy and is now housed in a Vanderbilt estate on Beachside Avenue. The seaside estates and beaches of Westport and Southport continue to line the cycling route to Southport Village Center.

A picnic lunch on the lawn beside the Southport Harbor and Yachting Club provides a pleasant and restful midday interlude.

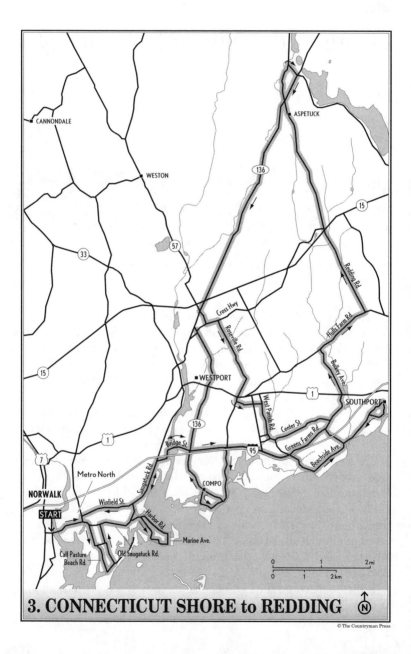

CANNONDALE

ASPETUCK

WESTON

136

15

33

57

Cross Hwy

Roseville Rd.

Redding Rd.

WESTPORT

Hulls Farm Rd.

15

1

Bulkley Ave.

SOUTHPORT

West Parish Rd.

Center St.

Greens Farms Rd.

136

95

Beachside Ave.

Bridge St.

1

7

Metro North

Saugatuck Rd.

COMPO

NORWALK

Winfield St.

START

Harbor Rd.

Marine Ave.

Call Pasture
Beach Rd.

Old Saugatuck Rd.

0   1   2 mi

0   1   2 km

3. CONNECTICUT SHORE to REDDING

N

© The Countryman Press

0.0	Turn right from Veterans Memorial Park onto Seaview Avenue
0.3	Turn right onto Cove Avenue
0.6	Turn left onto Fifth Street
0.8	Bear right onto Calf Pasture Beach Road
1.4	Turn left onto Canfield Avenue
1.6	Bear left at intersection onto Shorehaven Road
2.2	Turn right onto Pine Hill Avenue
2.6	Turn right onto Old Saugatuck Road (unmarked)
4.0	Turn right onto Harbor Road
4.2	Turn right onto Bermuda Road
	Bear left onto Surf Road (gravel for 40 yards)
	Turn right immediately onto Cockenoe Drive (unmarked)
	Turn left immediately onto Marine Avenue
	Turn left immediately onto Harbor Road
6.1	Turn right onto Duck Pond Road
6.5	Turn right onto CT 136/Saugatuck Road
7.5	Continue straight on CT 136 under railroad tracks, then right at light onto CT/136/Charles Street
7.7	Turn left onto Riverside Avenue
7.8	Turn right onto CT 136/Bridge Street
9.1	Go straight onto Greens Farms Road
10.5	Continue straight on Greens Farms Road past Clapboard Hill Road; Option begins here
11.0	Go straight across overpass onto Beachside Avenue (becomes New Creek Road/Pequot Road)
13.8	Arrive in Southport Village Center and turn right onto Main Street
14.1	Arrive at Southport Harbor
	Leave Southport Harbor and bear right onto Westway Road
14.4	Turn left onto Pequot Road
15.7	Bear right at Y intersection onto New Creek Road
16.4	Turn left at the end of New Creek Road onto Green's Farms Road and bear right to continue on Green's Farm Road
17.6	Turn left onto Hills Point Road (becomes Compo Road South)
19.5	Turn left onto Compo Beach Road at Minute Man statue, toward Compo Beach
	Leave Compo Beach on Soundview Drive
20.1	Turn left onto Compo Road South, passing Minuteman Statue
21.4	Turn left onto CT 136/Bridge Street
22.7	Turn left at the traffic light onto Riverside Avenue
22.8	Turn right onto CT 136/Charles Street
23.0	Turn left onto CT 136/Saugatuck Road (becomes Winfield Street)
24.1	Turn left onto East Avenue
24.6	Turn right onto Seaview Avenue
24.8	End tour at Veterans Memorial Park

Option (from mile 10.5)

0.0	Turn left onto Clapboard Hill Road
1.2	Go straight across Maple Avenue to continue on Clapboard Hill Road
1.5	Turn left onto Green's Farms Road (unmarked)
2.0	Turn left onto Bulkey Avenue south
2.2	Cross US 1/Post Road east onto Bulkey Avenue north
3.3	Turn right onto Hulls Farm Road (unmarked)
4.6	Turn left onto Redding Road
5.9	Bear left on Redding Road and continue straight as Old Redding Road bears left
10.5	Go straight across CT 136 to continue on Redding Road
10.9	Turn right onto Black Rock Turnpike (unmarked)
11.0	Turn right onto CT 136
15.2	Continue straight on CT 136/Easton Road across Redding Road
16.1	Turn left at blinking light onto Weston Road (unmarked)
16.5	Turn left onto Cross Highway
16.8	Turn right onto Roseville Road
18.5	Go straight across US 1/Post Road east
18.6	Turn left onto Hillandale Road
19.3	Turn right onto West Parish Road
19.6	Turn right onto Center Street
19.9	Turn left onto Green's Farms Road and continue from mile 11.0

Note that on Sunday the grocery stores and delis in Southport Village close early.

Park your bicycle at one of the bike racks at Westport's Campo Beach on the return ride and enjoy a swim. Changing facilities and bathrooms are located on the beach.

This ride involves a number of quick turns and the route can be a challenging one to follow. Check the directions frequently to avoid missing turns.

If you choose the optional ride to Redding, you'll discover that the countryside is quite characteristic of western Connecticut: The terrain here becomes wooded and rolling as the route passes small farms and the old stone walls that traditionally provided property markers here.

DRIVING DIRECTIONS   Take I-95 north into Connecticut. Leave I-95 at exit 16/East Norwalk. Turn right from the exit onto East Avenue and continue to the end, then turn right onto Sea View Avenue. Turn left into the first entrance to Veterans Memorial Park. You can park here or continue to the end of the road that goes through the park and turn right to park along the water, where there's a very scenic view of the bay and Long Island Sound.

Metro North's New Haven Line from Grand Central Station stops at the East Norwalk Station.

There is a bathroom in the small brick building on the right in Veterans Memorial Park.

Drive time from New York City is one hour.

RIDE DIRECTIONS

0.0 Leaving Veterans Memorial Park, turn right onto Seaview Avenue.
The parking area at the rear of the park adjacent to the water offers a scenic overlook of the bay and Long Island Sound.

0.3 Take the second right onto Cove Avenue.

0.6 Turn left onto Fifth Street.

0.8 The road curves right onto Calf Pasture Beach Road.

1.4 Turn left onto Canfield Avenue at the marina on the right.

1.6 Bear left onto Shorehaven Road at the intersection.
There's a golf course on the right at this point.

2.2 Turn right onto Pine Hill Avenue at the stop sign.

2.6 Turn right at the end of Pine Hill Avenue onto unmarked Old Saugatuck Road.

4.0 Turn right onto Harbor Road.
This part of the route has quite a few quick turns. The cycling takes you past a scenic waterfront subdivision of contemporary homes.

4.2 Turn right onto Bermuda Road.

Bear left immediately onto Surf Road (which is gravel for 40 yards).
You'll have to dismount and walk your bike here on the gravel part of Surf Road.

Turn right immediately onto unmarked Cockenoe Drive.

Readying for a refreshing break at the beach

Turn left immediately onto Marine Avenue.

Turn left immediately onto Harbor Road.

Walk across the small bridge to continue on Harbor Road.

6.1 Turn right at the end of Harbor Road onto Duck Pond Road.

6.5 Turn right at the end of Duck Pond Road onto CT 136/Saugatuck Road.

7.5 Go straight under the railroad tracks, following signs for CT 136 north, then right at the traffic light onto CT 136/Charles Street.

7.7 Turn left at the end of Charles Street onto Riverside Avenue.

7.8 Turn right onto CT 136/Bridge Street at the traffic light.
Peter's Bridge Market on the right at this turn is a good place to stop for fresh fruit, especially if you plan to ride the long Option, along which there are no services. It's always best to have some fruit or a sweet with you for an energy boost.

Continue across the bridge.
There is a pedestrian walkway on the left.

9.1 Go straight onto Green's Farms Road at the traffic light.

9.5 At the stop sign go straight to continue on Green's Farms Road.

9.9 Continue straight on Green's Farms Road at the traffic light.

10.5 Continue straight on Green's Farms Road, passing Clapboard Hill Road. The Option turns left here onto Clapboard Hill Road.

11.0 Go straight across the bridge onto Beachside Avenue (which becomes New Creek Road/Pequot Road) as Green's Farms Road veers to the left.
You'll pass Southport's beach. There are bathrooms at the beach, just beside the road.

13.8 Arrive in Southport Village Center and turn right onto Main Street.
There are a few delis here where you can purchase a sandwich. Note that there's only one deli open on Sunday, and it closes at 1:00 PM.

Cycle out of the village on Main Street.
You can usually use the bathroom at the firehouse on the left.

14.1 Arrive at Southport Harbor.

This is a lovely picnic spot on the lawn beside the Southport Yacht Club. There are no trash cans here, so you'll have to carry out your lunch wrappings.

To leave Southport Harbor, go to the left and bear right onto Westway Road.

14.4 Turn left onto Pequot Road at the stop sign.

15.7 Bear right onto unmarked New Creek Road at the Y intersection at the second stone bridge and continue under the railroad overpass.

16.4 Turn left at the end of New Creek Road onto Greens Farms Road, continue uphill, then bear right to continue on Greens Farms Road.

16.8 Go straight at the traffic light.

17.6 Turn left at the stop sign onto Hills Point Road.
Hills Point Road becomes South Compo Road. Follow the bike route signs leading to the beach. Don't enter the beach against one-way traffic!

19.5 Turn left at the Minute Man statue onto Compo Beach Road and follow it as it loops around to Compo Beach.
Compo Beach is a good place for a swim. There are changing facilities, bathrooms, and places to lock up your bicycle.

Following the traffic patterns, leave the beach area to the right onto Soundview Drive.

20.1 Turn left onto Compo Road South, passing the Minute Man Statue.

21.4 Turn left onto CT 136/Bridge Street at the traffic light.

22.7 After crossing the bridge, turn left at the traffic light onto Riverside Avenue.

22.8 Turn right onto CT 136/Charles Street.

23.0 Turn left onto CT 136/Saugatuck Road at the traffic light and go straight as Saugatuck Road becomes Winfield Street.

24.1 At the traffic light at the end of Winfield Street, turn left onto East Avenue.
Metro North's New Haven Line station is located at this turn.

24.6 Turn right at the end of East Avenue onto Sea View Avenue.

24.8 Turn left into Veterans Memorial Park to end the tour.

Option

0.0 From mile 10.5 turn left onto Clapboard Hill Road.
There's a short, steep climb here.

1.2 Go straight across Maple Avenue and the following intersection, continuing on Clapboard Hill Road.

1.5 Turn left at the end of Clapboard Hill Road onto unmarked Green's Farms Road.

2.0 Turn left onto Bulkey Avenue south.

2.2 Jog to the right across US 1/Post Road east onto Bulkey Avenue north.
On summer weekends seasonal polo matches are often held in the field on the left just before the turn onto Hulls Farm Road.

3.3 Turn right at the end of Bulkey Avenue onto unmarked Hulls Farm Road.

4.6 Turn left onto Redding Road at the stop sign.

5.9 Bear left at the stop sign to continue on Redding Road, then go straight on Redding Road as Old Redding Road bears left.

10.5 Go straight across unmarked CT 136 and continue on Redding Road at the stop sign.

10.9 Turn right at the end of Redding Road onto unmarked Black Rock Turnpike.
Bathrooms are available in the park on the left.

11.0 Turn right onto CT 136 south at the traffic light.

11.8 Go straight on CT 136, crossing Redding Road.
There's a nice downhill run here on CT 136.

15.2 Go straight on CT 136/Easton Road, crossing Redding Road.

16.1 Turn left at the blinking light after the overpass onto unmarked Weston Road.

16.5 Turn left at the end of Weston Road onto Cross Highway.

16.8 Turn right onto Roseville Road.
Be prepared for a few short, steep climbs here.

18.5 Go straight across US 1/Post Road east at the traffic light.
A McDonald's is located on the right, just before the light.

18.6 Take the first left after US 1 onto Hillandale Road.
Turn with the direction of traffic after passing the small dividing island in the road.

19.3 Turn right onto West Parish Road.

19.6 Turn right at the end of West Parish Road onto Center Street.

19.9 Make a hard left turn at the end of Center Street onto Green's Farms Road.
This will return you to the tour at mile 11.0.

NEW YORK

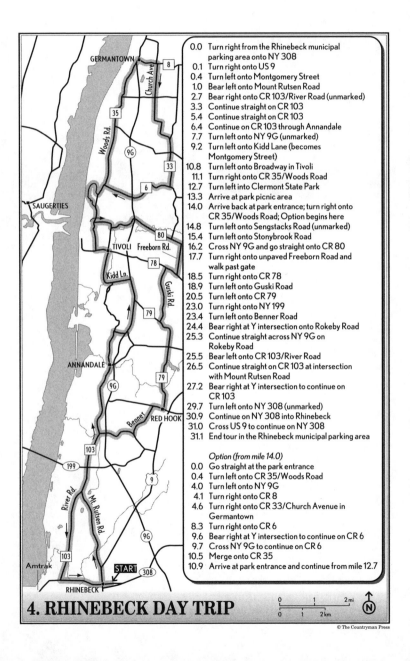

0.0	Turn right from the Rhinebeck municipal parking area onto NY 308
0.1	Turn right onto US 9
0.4	Turn left onto Montgomery Street
1.0	Bear left onto Mount Rutsen Road
2.7	Bear right onto CR 103/River Road (unmarked)
3.3	Continue straight on CR 103
5.4	Continue straight on CR 103
6.4	Continue on CR 103 through Annandale
7.7	Turn left onto NY 9G (unmarked)
9.2	Turn left onto Kidd Lane (becomes Montgomery Street)
10.8	Turn left onto Broadway in Tivoli
11.1	Turn right onto CR 35/Woods Road
12.7	Turn left into Clermont State Park
13.3	Arrive at park picnic area
14.0	Arrive back at park entrance; turn right onto CR 35/Woods Road; Option begins here
14.8	Turn left onto Sengstacks Road (unmarked)
15.4	Turn left onto Stonybrook Road
16.2	Cross NY 9G and go straight onto CR 80
17.7	Turn right onto unpaved Freeborn Road and walk past gate
18.5	Turn right onto CR 78
18.9	Turn left onto Guski Road
20.5	Turn left onto CR 79
23.0	Turn right onto NY 199
23.4	Turn left onto Benner Road
24.4	Bear right at Y intersection onto Rokeby Road
25.3	Continue straight across NY 9G on Rokeby Road
25.5	Bear left onto CR 103/River Road
26.5	Continue straight on CR 103 at intersection with Mount Rutsen Road
27.2	Bear right at Y intersection to continue on CR 103
29.7	Turn left onto NY 308 (unmarked)
30.9	Continue on NY 308 into Rhinebeck
31.0	Cross US 9 to continue on NY 308
31.1	End tour in the Rhinebeck municipal parking area

Option (from mile 14.0)

0.0	Go straight at the park entrance
0.4	Turn left onto CR 35/Woods Road
4.0	Turn left onto NY 9G
4.1	Turn right onto CR 8
4.6	Turn right onto CR 33/Church Avenue in Germantown
8.3	Turn right onto CR 6
9.6	Bear right at Y intersection to continue on CR 6
9.7	Cross NY 9G to continue on CR 6
10.5	Merge onto CR 35
10.9	Arrive at park entrance and continue from mile 12.7

4. RHINEBECK DAY TRIP

0   1   2 mi
0   1   2 km

N

© The Countryman Press

Rhinebeck Day Trip

- **TOUR DISTANCE:** 31 miles (42 miles with Option)
- **TERRAIN:** Moderate, with rolling terrain throughout
- **SPECIAL FEATURES:** Rhinebeck Village, Clermont State Park

This ride has so many great features that it's been one of our most popular one-day trips for many years. Rhinebeck Village is noted for a casual style of elegance and a history that dates back more than three hundred years. The ride explores the peaceful valleys of northern Dutchess County and is lined with fruit orchards, historic riverfront estates, and impressive views of the Hudson River.

Amtrak trains departing from New York's Penn Station stop at the Rhinecliff Train Station, which is just 2 miles from Rhinebeck Village. You'll encounter a little bit of traffic leaving the village, but shortly the route leads you to the gently rolling terrain of River Road, paralleling the Hudson River. The route passes Montgomery Place, a meticulously restored Hudson River estate that has landscaped grounds and gardens; nature trails; and orchards, where you can enjoy seasonal fruit picking. The riding continues past the campus of Bard College in Annandale, where the new Frank Gehry–designed concert hall is located. Just before you arrive in the quaint village of Tivoli, you can enjoy wonderful views of the Catskill Mountains to the west. Although it's possible to have a full-service lunch in Tivoli, purchasing a sandwich and pedaling 2 miles to Clermont State Park for lunch is a wonderful choice. The park's picnic grounds are located on a bluff with rolling lawns

A handsome barn in the Hudson Valley countryside

sweeping down to the banks of the Hudson River. There's a grand view of the river and the Catskill Mountains, making lunch here a pleasant pause. The Clermont Estate is located just beside the picnic area; if time allows, enjoy a visit to the gardens or the galleries of this historic site. Clermont, once encompassing an area of 16,000 acres in Columbia County, is the oldest of the riverfront estates in the mid–Hudson Valley. Robert R. Livingston, the great-grandson of the patriarch of the estate, was a signer of the Declaration of Independence and a negotiator of the Louisiana Purchase.

A highly recommended 11-mile Option loops out into Columbia County and back to the park, leading through a very pastoral and picturesque part of this area.

Enjoy exploring Rhinebeck's cafés and shops on Main Street at the completion of the ride. Worth noting is that there's often a farmer's market on Saturday morning in the municipal parking area across from the firehouse. The history of Rhinebeck is described in more detail in tour 5, Clinton to Rhinebeck.

DRIVING DIRECTIONS   Take the Henry Hudson Parkway to the Saw Mill River Parkway. Continue on the Saw Mill Parkway to the Taconic State Parkway north. Exit the Taconic State Parkway at NY 199/Pine Plains and Red Hook. Turn left onto NY 199 west toward Rhinebeck. Follow NY 199 for 10 miles, then continue straight onto NY 308 toward Rhinebeck. Follow NY 308 into Rhinebeck Village. Park in the municipal parking area on the right, opposite the Rhinebeck Fire Department.

Amtrak trains leaving Penn Station in New York City stop at the Rhinecliff Train Station, which is 2.2 miles from Rhinebeck Village. Follow NY 308 east from the train station to the village.

There is a portable bathroom in the municipal parking area, and there are bathroom facilities in the restaurants on Main Street.

Drive time from New York City is two hours.

RIDE DIRECTIONS

0.0 Turn right from the municipal parking area onto NY 308.

0.1 Turn right onto US 9 north toward Red Hook.

0.4 Turn left onto Montgomery Street.
This turn occurs just before you reach the hospital as US 9 curves right.

1.0 Bear left and continue uphill on Mount Rutsen Road.

2.7 Bear right onto unmarked CR 103 north/River Road.
The road here curves right at the yield sign.

3.3 Continue straight on CR 103 north at the traffic light.
The route passes the entrance to Montgomery Place on the Hudson on the left, where there are nature trails and also seasonal fruit picking.

5.4 Continue straight at the stop sign, remaining on CR 103 north.

6.4 Follow CR 103 north as it curves left and then right into Annandale.

To visit the new Frank Gehry–designed concert hall at Bard College, take the lane on the left just after the route turns right and starts climbing. This will lead onto the campus and eventually to the concert hall.

7.7 Turn left at the stop sign onto unmarked NY 9G north.
This road has some faster-moving traffic; however, there's an adequate shoulder for cyclists.

9.2 Turn left onto Kidd Lane (becomes Montgomery Street), which is the first left after CR 79.
Enjoy the lovely views of the Catskill Mountains to the west.

10.8 In the village of Tivoli turn left onto Broadway.
Tivoli is located at the intersection of Montgomery Street and CR 78. There's a restaurant in the village, but I suggest purchasing a sandwich and enjoying a picnic lunch at Clermont State Park.

11.1 Take the second right onto Woods Road.

12.7 Turn left into Clermont State Park.
Enjoy a picnic lunch stop here. The park's lawn rolls down to the Hudson River, and there's a tour available of the Livingston Homestead, which is adjacent to the picnic area. There are bathrooms at the picnic area, but because this is a carry in/carry out park, there is no place to deposit trash. The Option starts and finishes at the park entrance.

13.3 Reverse direction after lunch and cycle to the park entrance.

14.0 At the park entrance turn right onto Woods Road.
The Option begins here.

14.8 Take the first left onto unmarked Sengstacks Road.
Keep an eye on your mileage here; it's easy to miss this unmarked road.

15.4 Turn left at the end of Sengstacks Road onto Stonybrook Road.

16.2 Go straight across NY 9G onto CR 80.

17.7 Turn right onto Freeborn Road.
Walk bikes around the gate at the ROAD CLOSED sign. Freeborn Lane is unpaved for about 0.5 mile.

18.5 Turn right at the end of Freeborn Road onto CR 78.

18.9 Take the first left onto Guski Road.

20.5 Turn left at the end of Guski Road onto CR 79.
Be careful at this intersection, which you approach on a downhill across traffic on the right that's difficult to see.

23.0 Turn right onto NY 199 west at the stop sign.
The center of the village of Red Hook is just to the left at this turn.

23.4 Turn left onto Benner Road.

24.4 Bear right at the Y intersection onto Rokeby Road.

25.3 Continue straight on Rokeby Road, crossing NY 9G.

25.5 Bear left onto CR 103 south/River Road at the stop sign.
From this point on the directions reverse the route taken to leave Rhinebeck.

26.5 Continue straight on CR 103 at the traffic light and the intersection with Mount Rutsen Road.

27.2 Bear right at Y intersection to remain on CR 103 south.

29.7 Turn left onto unmarked NY 308 east at the stop sign.
A right turn here leads to the village of Rhinecliff, 1 mile from this point. Turn right onto Hutton Street in Rhinecliff to visit the town park located on the banks of the Hudson River. Reverse direction when leaving the park to return to Rhinebeck.

30.9 Follow NY 308 east into Rhinebeck.

31.0 Go straight across US 9 at the traffic light to continue on NY 308.

31.1 Turn left into the municipal parking area to end the tour.

Option

0.0 From mile 14.0 go straight at the park entrance and follow the road as it curves right.
The directions here suggest riding the Option before lunch. But if you choose to take it after lunch, turn to the left onto NY 35 north when reaching the park entrance. This optional loop covers fairly gentle terrain, is quite scenic and lightly traveled, and is highly recommended. The ride crosses into Columbia County at Clermont State Park.

0.4 Take the first left onto CR 35/Woods Road.

4.0 Turn left onto NY 9G north at the stop sign.

4.1 Turn right onto CR 8 at the traffic light.
There are convenience stores at this intersection.

4.6 Turn right onto CR 33 south/Church Avenue in Germantown.
There may be a restaurant at this turn. One has opened, closed, and then reopened through the years here.

8.3 Turn right at the end of Church Avenue onto CR 6 west.
This is Hudson Valley orchard country. Look for a small farm on the left along this road. At times there are reindeer here.

9.6 Bear right at the Y intersection to continue on CR 6.
Enjoy the beautiful views of the Catskills at the top of a short climb.

9.7 Go straight across NY 9G to remain on CR 6.

10.5 Merge onto CR 35 south.

10.9 Arrive at the entrance to Clermont State Park. Continue from mile 12.7.

5

Clinton to Rhinebeck

- **TOUR DISTANCE:** 27 miles (35 miles with Option 1, 46 miles with Options 1 and 2)
- **TERRAIN:** Moderate, with rolling terrain throughout and a few short steep climbs. Option 1 is easy; Option 2 is moderate, with rolling terrain throughout.
- **SPECIAL FEATURES:** Rhinebeck Village

The Hudson River Valley sweeps northward from New York City between the Palisades, Shawangunks, and Hudson Highlands to the west, and the Taconic Hills and Berkshires to the east. From its name—Hudson, after the 16th-century English navigator and explorer who sailed this river—visitors would expect to discover an area that has deep roots in early American history, which this region certainly has. With 437 sites listed on the National Register of Historic Places and 30 contiguous riverfront estates associated with the landed aristocracy of the 18th through the 20th centuries, the Hudson River Valley is a superb area not only for discovery, but also for a day or more of bicycling.

The ride starts in the hamlet of Clinton, nestled in the lush rolling hills of Dutchess County. Cyclists pedal on country lanes and well-paved roads, though there is a 0.4-mile section of good hard-packed road surface on Pumpkin Lane. Heading north and west toward the village of Rhinebeck, at mile 6.9, the road climbs on Salisbury Turnpike, where there are some rewarding views of the Catskill Mountains.

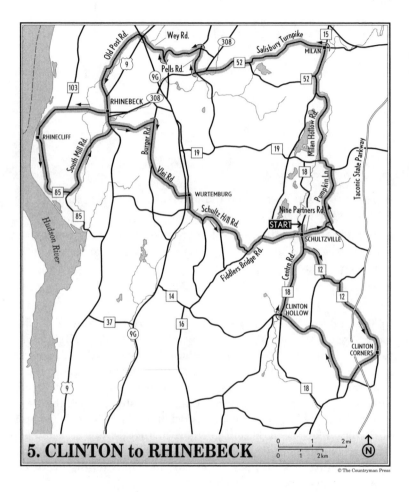

5. CLINTON to RHINEBECK

0   1   2 mi
0   1   2 km

N

© The Countryman Press

```
  0.0  Turn right from Clinton Town Offices parking area onto NY 18/Centre Road
  0.4  Turn left onto Nine Partners Road
  1.1  Bear left on Nine Partners Road at Y intersection
  1.3  Turn left onto Pumpkin Lane
  2.9  Continue straight across CR 19/Bulls Head Road
  3.0  Turn left onto Old Bulls Head Road
  3.4  Turn right onto CR 15/Milan Hollow Road
  6.1  Bear right on CR 15/Milan Hollow Road
  6.9  Turn left onto Salisbury Turnpike
  9.5  Continue on Salisbury Turnpike as it merges with CR 52
 10.8  Turn left onto NY 308 (unmarked)
 11.0  Turn right onto Pells Road
 11.8  Turn left onto Cedar Heights Road
 12.8  Bear left on Cedar Heights Road at intersection with Crosby Lane
 13.1  Turn right onto Wey Road (unmarked)
 14.1  Go straight across US 9 onto Old Post Road
 14.2  Cross NY 9G on Old Post Road
 15.9  Turn left onto Montgomery Street (unmarked)
 16.5  Turn right onto US 9 (unmarked)
 17.0  Arrive in Rhinebeck and turn left onto NY 308/East Market Street; Option 1 begins here
        Leave Rhinebeck by reversing direction and turning left onto US 9
 17.4  Turn left onto Asher Road
 17.5  Turn right onto Huntington Road
 17.8  Go straight onto Knollwood Road
 19.0  Turn right onto Burger Road
 20.2  Go straight onto Ackert Hook Road
 20.4  Go straight onto Vlei Road
 21.9  Go straight across NY 9G to continue on Vlei Road
 22.0  Turn right onto Wurtemburg Road
 22.4  Turn left onto Schultz Hill Road
 22.9  Bear left at intersection to continue on Schultz Hill Road
 24.9  Turn left onto Fiddler's Bridge Road
 26.7  Turn left onto Centre Road; Option 2 begins here
 27.1  End tour at Clinton Town Offices parking area


        Option 1 (from mile 17.0)
  0.0  Continue on NY 308/West Market Street in Rhinebeck (becomes Rhinecliff Road)
  1.2  Continue straight past River Road
  2.2  Turn right onto Hutton Street toward River Front Park
        Leave River Front Park by reversing direction on Hutton Street
  2.5  Turn right onto Charles Street
  2.6  Continue straight onto Kelly Street/CR 85/Morton Road
  5.0  Turn left onto South Mill Road
  7.4  Turn left onto US 9
  7.9  Turn right onto East Market Street and continue from mile 17.0


        Option 2 (from mile 26.7)
  0.0  Turn right onto CR 18/Centre Road
  0.4  Turn left onto CR 12/Clinton Corners Road/Schultzville Road
  0.7  Hard-packed surface begins
  1.5  Turn left to continue on CR 12/Clinton Corners Road/ Schultzville Road (unmarked)
  2.6  Pass Clinton Vineyards on right
  3.9  Turn right onto CR 17/Salt Point Turnpike (unmarked)
  4.4  Arrive at Jeanie Bean's store
  5.5  Turn right onto CR 14/Hollow Road
  8.7  Turn right onto CR 18/Centre Road
 11.0  Continue straight past Fiddler's Bridge Road to end in Clinton Town Offices parking area
```

Rhinebeck Village was founded in 1686 as a result of a land transaction of 2,200 acres among four Dutchmen and the Esopus and Sepasco Indian tribes. The village was originally known as Kipsbergen, but in 1713 it was renamed Ryn Beck after Henry Beekman, a wealthy judge who resided there. The Beekman Arms Hotel, which sits at the town's main intersection of NY 308 and US 9, has been welcoming travelers since it opened in 1766 and is now considered to be the oldest inn in America. There are some cafés on NY 308 offering good lunch options. If time permits, enjoy browsing through the local shops.

Option 1 is an easy 8-mile loop out from Rhinebeck to the Town Landing Park in Rhinecliff and back to Rhinebeck. While in the park, stop and enjoy the wonderful views across the Hudson River. Amtrak trains departing from New York's Penn Station stop at the Rhinecliff Train Station. The pedaling on Option 2 is all on quiet country lanes. The route passes Clinton Vineyards, which is listed on the Dutchess County Wine Trail, and leads through the hamlet of Clinton Corners, where on weekends Jeanie Bean's Country Store serves up traditional English fare. It's a good stop for ambience and also for some tea and scones with clotted cream.

DRIVING DIRECTIONS   Take the Henry Hudson Parkway to the Saw Mill River Parkway. From the Saw Mill Parkway take the exit just after Hawthorne to the Taconic State Parkway north, continuing into Dutchess County. Exit the Taconic State Parkway by carefully turning left across the parkway onto Pumpkin Lane, just after the turnoff for Willow Lane. Continue straight onto Electronic Lane as Pumpkin Lane goes off to the right. Turn left onto Nine Partners Road at the stop sign. Turn right onto Centre Road at the stop sign and continue 0.4 mile to the Clinton Town Offices. Turn left into the driveway and park on the circular driveway in front of the building.

Amtrak trains leaving Penn Station in New York City stop at the Rhinecliff Train Station, which is located at the 2.2-mile mark on Option 1.

There are bathrooms at the Schultzville General Store, which is located just beyond the stop sign before turning right onto Centre Road.

Drive time from New York City is 1 hour and 30 minutes.

RIDE DIRECTIONS

0.0 Leaving the Clinton Town Offices parking area, turn right onto NY 18/Centre Road.

0.4 Turn left onto Nine Partners Road.
The Schultzville General Store is on the right at this turn.

1.1 Bear left at the Y intersection to continue on Nine Partners Road.

1.3 Turn left onto Pumpkin Lane.
There's 0.4 mile of good hard-packed road surface here.

2.9 Continue straight across unmarked CR 19/Bull's Head Road.

3.0 Turn left onto Old Bull's Head Road.

3.4 Turn right onto CR 15/Milan Hollow Road.
There's a steady climb here.

6.1 Bear right to continue on CR 15 north/Milan Hollow Road.

6.9 Turn left onto Salisbury Turnpike.
After a short but steep climb there's a beautiful view of the Catskill Mountains to the west.

9.5 Continue on Salisbury Turnpike as it merges straight with CR 52.

10.8 Turn left at the end of Salisbury Turnpike onto unmarked NY 308.
Be careful of traffic for 0.2 mile.

11.0 Turn right onto Pells Road.

11.8 Turn left onto Cedar Heights Road.

12.8 Bear left on Cedar Heights Road at the intersection with Crosby Lane.

13.1 Turn right at the end of Cedar Heights Road onto unmarked Wey Road.

14.1 Go straight across US 9 onto Old Post Road.

14.2 Jog to the right and then to the left across NY 9G on Old Post Road.

15.9 Turn left at the end of Old Post Road onto unmarked Montgomery Street.

16.5 Turn right at the end of Montgomery Street onto unmarked US 9.

17.0 Arrive in Rhinebeck and turn left at the traffic light onto NY 308/East Market Street.
Take some time to explore the village of Rhinebeck. The historic Beekman Arms Inn, which offers a full-service lunch, is on the right at the intersection of US 9 and NY 308. The inn's old pub and restaurant are part of the original structure and are definitely worth a look. There are some other good lunch choices just after the left turn on NY 308, and there's often a farmer's market on Saturday in the municipal parking area across the street from the firehouse. At mile 17.0 Option 1 loops out to Rhinecliff and back to Rhinebeck.

Leaving Rhinebeck, turn left onto US 9 south at the traffic light.

17.4 Turn left onto Asher Road.

17.5 Turn right onto Huntington Road.

17.8 Go straight onto Knollwood Road.

19.0 Turn right at the end of Knollwood Road onto Burger Road.

20.2 Go straight onto Ackert Hook Road.

20.4 Go straight onto Vlei Road.

21.9 Go straight across NY 9G to continue on Vlei Road.
Be careful of the fast-moving traffic on NY 9G.

22.0 Turn right at the end of Vlei Road onto Wurtemburg Road.

22.4 Turn left at the end of Wurtemburg Road onto Schultz Hill Road.
There's a steep uphill here.

22.9 Bear left at the intersection to continue on Schultz Hill Road.
The climb continues.

24.9 Turn left at the end of Schultz Hill Road (at the church) onto Fiddler's Bridge Road.

Fall is a great time to bike in the Hudson Valley

26.7 Turn left onto Centre Road at the Schultzville Store.
Option 2 turns right here onto Centre Road.

27.1 Turn left into the Clinton Town Offices parking area to end tour.

Option 1

0.0 From mile 17.0 continue straight at the traffic light onto NY 308/West Market Street (becomes Rhinecliff Road).

1.2 Continue straight on West Market Street, passing River Road on the right.

2.2 Turn right onto Hutton Street and continue to River Front Park.
The park offers wonderful views across the Hudson River to the Catskill Mountains. This is a good place to enjoy a picnic if you can carry your lunch with you. Leave the park by reversing direction and returning to Hutton Street. Amtrak's train from Penn Station in New York City stops at River Front Park.

2.5 Turn right onto Charles Street.

2.6 Continue straight onto Kelly Street/CR 85/Morton Road.

5.0 Turn left onto South Mill Road.

7.4 Turn left at the end of South Mill Road onto US 9.
Take care here; there's some traffic entering Rhinebeck Village.

7.9 Turn right onto East Market Street at the traffic light.
Continue from mile 17.0.

Option 2

0.0 From mile 26.7 turn right at the Schultzville Store onto CR 18/Centre Road.

0.4 Turn left onto CR 12/Clinton Corners Road/Schultzville Road.

0.7 Good hard-packed road surface begins.

1.5 Turn left to continue on unmarked CR 12/Clinton Corners Road/Schultzville Road.
The hard-packed road surface ends here.

2.6 Pass Clinton Vineyards on the right.

3.9 Turn right onto unmarked CR 17/Salt Point Turnpike.

4.4 Arrive at Jeanie Bean's Store.
Stop here for tea and scones. The ambience is quite unique.

5.5 Turn right onto CR 14/Hollow Road.
The pedaling is uphill at the beginning of this road and then downhill before the turn onto Centre Road.

8.7 Turn right onto CR 18/Centre Road.

11.0 Continue straight, passing Fiddler's Bridge Road, to end in the Clinton Town Offices parking area.

6

Millbrook to Clinton Corners

- **TOUR DISTANCE:** 31 miles (39 miles with Option 1; 48 miles with Options 1 and 2)
- **TERRAIN:** Moderate, with rolling terrain throughout and a few short, steep climbs
- **SPECIAL FEATURES:** Institute of Ecosystem Studies, Millbrook Village, Millbrook Vineyards

The secondary roads and country lanes that meander through Dutchess County, New York, make it quite easy to plan a number of varied cycling itineraries that bring the rider close to natural surroundings. Picturesque horse farms and fruit orchards line these routes, interspersed with charming villages and local seasonal flea markets.

The Institute of Ecosystems Studies, located in Millbrook, is the starting point for this ride. Because the institute offers courses throughout the year that attract a good deal of interest, it may be best to call ahead to insure that their parking area is available for cyclists' use. The institute occupies 1,924 acres and was once the country home of Mary Flagler, who was the beneficiary of a part of the Standard Oil fortune. Today the New York Botanical Gardens acts as the custodian of the site. Its mission is to foster scientific and educational programs that maintain and preserve our natural resources. If time permits, a walk through the institute's gardens or on one of its many trails makes for a delightful break.

The first part of this ride is marked by gracious country homes

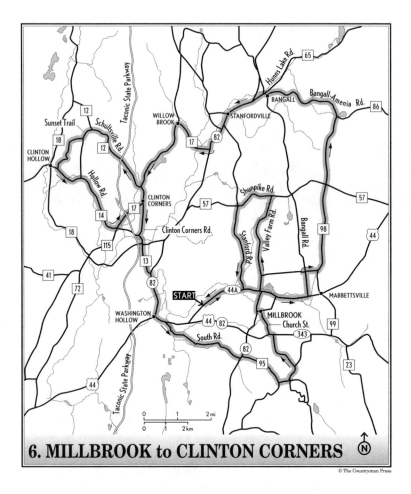

6. MILLBROOK to CLINTON CORNERS

0.0 Turn left onto NY 44A from Institute for Ecosystems Studies parking area
2.2 Continue straight onto US 44
3.1 Turn left onto Bangall Road
3.9 Turn right onto Daheim Road
4.3 Turn left onto CR 98
6.9 Go straight across CR 57 to continue on CR 98 (becomes Shuman Road)
8.9 Bear left onto Bangall-Amenia Road (unmarked)
11.5 Turn left onto CR 65/Hunns Lake Road
12.0 Merge straight onto NY 82
13.9 Turn right onto CR 17
17.6 Continue on CR 17 into Clinton Corners; Option 1 begins here
18.0 Leave Clinton Corners on CR 13/Clinton Corners Road
19.0 Bear left to continue on CR 13
20.2 Turn right onto NY 82
21.5 Turn left onto NY 82/US 44
21.8 Turn right onto South Road
23.0 Bear left at intersection with Verbank Road to continue on South Road
24.6 Turn left onto NY 82
24.7 Turn right immediately onto CR 95/Oak Summit Road
26.1 Bear left at Y intersection onto CR 96
28.2 Turn left onto NY 343
28.3 Turn right onto Church Street
29.0 Arrive in Millbrook at intersection of Church Street and Franklin Street
   Turn left immediately onto Franklin Street
   Turn right immediately onto Front Street (becomes Harts Village Road)
29.6 Turn left onto NY 44A
29.7 Pass Valley Farm Road; Option 2 begins here
31.3 End tour at Institute for Ecosystem Studies parking area

Option 1 (from mile 17.6)
0.0 Turn right onto Schultzville Road/Clinton Corners Road
2.5 Go straight onto unpaved Sunset Trail
2.9 Bear right at fork to continue on Sunset Trail
3.3 Turn left to continue on Sunset Trail
4.3 Turn left onto CR 14/Hollow Road
7.2 Turn left onto NY 115 (becomes CR 17)
7.8 Pass the Stewart's Convenience Store
8.3 End in Clinton Corners and continue from mile 17.6

Option 2 (from mile 29.7)
0.0 Turn right onto Valley Farm Road
3.0 Turn left onto CR 57/Shunpike Road
4.5 Turn left onto Stanford Road
7.0 Turn right onto NY 44A
8.1 End at Institute for Ecosystems Studies parking area

and idyllic views of the surrounding countryside. The terrain is rolling for the first 9 miles, with a short unpaved section on Daheim Road. The hamlet of Bangall has a country store that's definitely worth a stop. As you enter Bangall on the right, you'll notice the sign that reads JAMES CAGNEY WAY. This area was where the famous actor had his vacation home. The cycling from Bangall to Clinton Corners becomes gentler. In late spring to early summer it's common to see flea markets beside the road as the ride passes through Stanfordville. Jeanie Bean's Country Store in Clinton Corners provides a wonderful full-service lunch with an English flair, but note that it's open only on the weekends. After lunch the ride leads through the center of Millbrook, an attractive Hudson Valley village that offers opportunities to browse antiques shops or stop for an ice cream cone. Note that some of the stores in Millbrook are closed on Sunday.

There are two Options on this ride: The loop out of Clinton Corners is quite hilly but is extremely quiet and scenic, while Option 2 comprises rolling terrain that leads to Millbrook Vineyards. Founded in 1981 and now occupying 130 acres, the vineyard offers tours and tasting and has produced some higher quality Hudson Valley wines.

DRIVING DIRECTIONS   Take the Henry Hudson Parkway north to the Saw Mill Parkway north. Continue on to the Taconic Parkway north. Exit the Taconic Parkway at US 44 in Dutchess County. Turn right onto US 44 toward Millbrook. After 1.8 miles turn left onto NY 44A. After 1 mile turn left into the second entrance to the Institute for Ecosystem Studies parking area (marked Gifford House/Visitors Center/Gift Shop). Park at the rear of the parking area.

There are bathrooms in the gift shop on weekdays and Saturday.

Drive time from New York City is 1 hour and 25 minutes.

RIDE DIRECTIONS

0.0 Turn left from the Institute for Ecosystems Studies parking area onto NY 44A.

2.2 Continue straight onto US 44 at the stop sign.

3.1 Turn left onto Bangall Road.
This turn occurs at the top of a short climb. Watch carefully for it; the signpost is on the left.

3.9 Turn right onto Daheim Road.
This road is unpaved.

4.3 Turn left at the end of Daheim Road onto CR 98.
There are beautiful views of meadows, valleys, and horse farms on this rolling section of the ride all the way to the hamlet of Bangall.

6.9 Go straight across CR 57 onto CR 98 (which becomes Shuman Road).

8.9 Bear left onto unmarked Bangall-Amenia Road at the yield sign.

11.5 Turn left onto CR 65/Hunns Lake Road.
The Bangall Store is definitely worth a stop for either a sandwich or a cold drink. They have a bathroom available.

12.0 Merge straight onto NY 82.
There's some traffic on this road, which passes Stanfordville. On weekends during the summer there's usually a flea market beside the road.

13.9 Turn right onto CR 17.

17.6 Pass Schultzville Road as CR 17 curves left into Clinton Corners.
Turn right onto Schultzville Road for Option 1.

18.0 Arrive at Jeanie Bean's Store.
For a full-service lunch, you can't beat the ambience here. For a picnic lunch, continue past the store for 0.3 mile to Friends Park on the left. There are usually a picnic table and a portable bathroom in the park.

Leave Clinton Corners on CR 13/Clinton Corners Road opposite Jeanie Bean's Store.

19.0 Bear left to continue on CR 13.

20.2 Turn right onto NY 82.

21.5 Turn left onto NY 82/US 44 east.
Be careful here; there's some traffic on this road.

21.8 Turn right onto South Road.

23.0 Bear left at the intersection with Verbank Road to continue on South Road.

24.6 Turn left onto NY 82 at the end of South Road.

24.7 Turn right immediately onto CR 95/Oak Summit Road.
Don't turn right onto the private, unpaved road!

26.1 Bear left at the Y intersection onto CR 96.
There's a short, steep uphill here, followed by a pleasant view of the Catskill Mountains.

28.2 Turn left onto NY 343.

28.3 Take the first right onto Church Street.

Jeanie Bean's serves up traditional English fare.

29.0 Arrive in Millbrook at the intersection of Church and Franklin Streets.
Take some time for an ice cream break or for browsing in the antiques shops on the main street.

Leaving Millbrook, turn left onto Franklin Street.

Turn right immediately onto Front Street, which becomes Harts Village Road.
A service station is located on the corner here.

29.6 At the end of Harts Village Road, go left onto NY 44A at the stop sign.

29.7 Pass Valley Farm Road.
Turn right onto Valley Farm Road for Option 2.

31.3 Turn right into the parking area for the Institute for Ecosystem Studies to end the tour.

Option 1

0.0 From mile 17.6 turn right onto Schultzville Road/Clinton Corners Road just before reaching Clinton Corners.
This rolling route passes Clinton Vineyards on the left on Schultzville Road.

2.5 Go straight onto unpaved Sunset Trail.
Slow down here; the pavement becomes bumpy and the road is scenic.

2.9 Bear right at the fork to continue on Sunset Trail.

3.3 Turn left to continue on Sunset Trail.

4.3 Turn left at the end of Sunset Trail onto CR 14/Hollow Road.

7.2 Turn left onto NY 115 (which becomes CR 17).

7.8 Pass Stewarts convenience store.

8.3 Arrive at Jeanie Bean's Store in Clinton Corners.
Continue from mile 17.6.

Option 2

0.0 From mile 29.7 turn right onto Valley Farm Road.
This Option is rolling throughout.

3.0 Turn left at the end of Valley Farm Road onto CR 57/Shunpike Road.
To visit Millbrook Vineyards, turn right onto CR 57/Shunpike Road, and then left onto Wing Road. After 0.1 mile on Wing Road, turn right into Millbrook Vineyards for 0.5 mile on a gravel road. Reverse direction when leaving the vineyard, returning to CR 57.

4.5 Turn left onto Stanford Road.

7.0 Turn right onto NY 44A at the stop sign.

8.1 Turn right into the parking area of the Institute for Ecosystem Studies.

Dutchess County, Northeast

- **TOUR DISTANCE:** 40 miles (50 miles with Option)
- **TERRAIN:** Moderate, with rolling terrain throughout and a few short, steep climbs
- **SPECIAL FEATURES:** Harlem Valley Rail Trail, Millerton

Farmland with rolling pastures, beaver ponds, and woodlands are the hallmarks of this one-day tour through northeastern Dutchess County. Pedaling on a section of the paved Harlem Valley Rail Trail offers an opportunity to observe a variety of animal and plant life in their undisturbed habitat.

The ride leaves from the Dover Plains Railroad Station (a stop for Metro North's Harlem Valley Rail Line), where parking is available on the weekends. Rolling terrain leads cyclists through the hamlet of Wassaic, located at the northern terminus of Metro North's Harlem Valley Rail Line. In 1831 the rail line received its charter, with a route intended to connect towns in Westchester, Putnam, and lower Dutchess County to New York City. By the early 1850s the Harlem Line had revenues of one million dollars a year, carrying commuters to Brewster and commercial freight between New York City and the outlying villages and farms to the north. In 1989 New York State purchased 22 miles of the right-of-way from Wassaic to Copake Falls in Columbia County, with the intent to create a linear park for cyclists, walkers, runners, and cross-country skiers. The Harlem Valley Rail Trail will eventually be a 46-mile linear park extending from the train station at

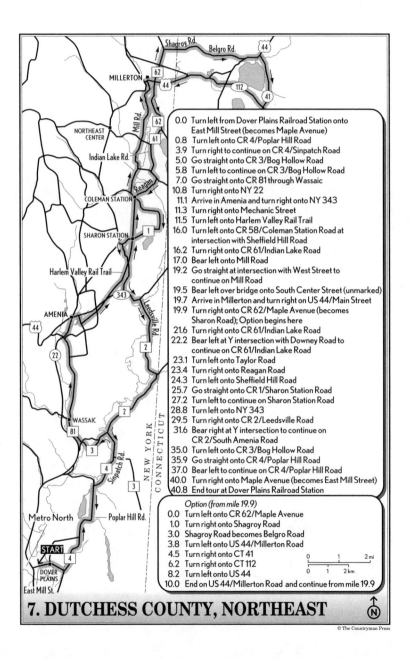

0.0 Turn left from Dover Plains Railroad Station onto East Mill Street (becomes Maple Avenue)
0.8 Turn left onto CR 4/Poplar Hill Road
3.9 Turn right to continue on CR 4/Sinpatch Road
5.0 Go straight onto CR 3/Bog Hollow Road
5.8 Turn left to continue on CR 3/Bog Hollow Road
7.0 Go straight onto CR 81 through Wassaic
10.8 Turn right onto NY 22
11.1 Arrive in Amenia and turn right onto NY 343
11.3 Turn right onto Mechanic Street
11.5 Turn left onto Harlem Valley Rail Trail
16.0 Turn left onto CR 58/Coleman Station Road at intersection with Sheffield Hill Road
16.2 Turn right onto CR 61/Indian Lake Road
17.0 Bear left onto Mill Road
19.2 Go straight at intersection with West Street to continue on Mill Road
19.5 Bear left over bridge onto South Center Street (unmarked)
19.7 Arrive in Millerton and turn right on US 44/Main Street
19.9 Turn right onto CR 62/Maple Avenue (becomes Sharon Road); Option begins here
21.6 Turn right onto CR 61/Indian Lake Road
22.2 Bear left at Y intersection with Downey Road to continue on CR 61/Indian Lake Road
23.1 Turn left onto Taylor Road
23.4 Turn right onto Reagan Road
24.3 Turn left onto Sheffield Hill Road
25.7 Go straight onto CR 1/Sharon Station Road
27.2 Turn left to continue on Sharon Station Road
28.8 Turn left onto NY 343
29.5 Turn right onto CR 2/Leedsville Road
31.6 Bear right at Y intersection to continue on CR 2/South Amenia Road
35.0 Turn left onto CR 3/Bog Hollow Road
35.9 Go straight onto CR 4/Poplar Hill Road
37.0 Bear left to continue on CR 4/Poplar Hill Road
40.0 Turn right onto Maple Avenue (becomes East Mill Street)
40.8 End tour at Dover Plains Railroad Station

Option (from mile 19.9)
0.0 Turn left onto CR 62/Maple Avenue
1.0 Turn right onto Shagroy Road
3.0 Shagroy Road becomes Belgro Road
3.8 Turn left onto US 44/Millerton Road
4.5 Turn right onto CT 41
6.2 Turn right onto CT 112
8.2 Turn left onto US 44
10.0 End on US 44/Millerton Road and continue from mile 19.9

7. DUTCHESS COUNTY, NORTHEAST

Wassaic in Dutchess County to the village of Chatham in Columbia County. The section of the trail on this cycling route has a pleasant grade and is paved for 8 miles, from Amenia to the village of Millerton. The old railroad station in Millerton adjacent to the trail seems to have changed little since the days when it was the focus of village activity.

The 10-mile optional loop starts and ends in Millerton and crosses the state line to Lakeville, Connecticut.

Leaving Millerton, the rolling terrain passes many larger Dutchess County dairy farms and offers pleasant views of the countryside. At mile 31.6 of the ride, a right turn is called for at a Y intersection in the center of the hamlet of Amenia Union. The stone boundary pillar standing in the triangle at the Y intersection marks the state line between New York and Connecticut. Just to the left, 0.1 mile before the left turn onto NY 4/Popular Hill Road, is the World Peace Sanctuary Park, where a rally for world peace is held each year.

DRIVING DIRECTIONS   Take the Henry Hudson Parkway to the Saw Mill Parkway and the Sawmill Parkway to I-684 north. Continue on I-684 to the end and then go straight onto NY 22 north, which becomes NY 22 north/NY 55 east. After 18 miles continue on NY 22 north as it curves to the left. After 7 additional miles turn right toward the Dover Plains Train Station at the traffic light in Dover Plains just before the Citgo gas station. Turn left just before the railroad tracks and drive into the rear parking area of the Metro North Dover Plains Railroad Station. Parking is available here on weekends, and the ride starts and finishes here. Trains to this location depart from Grand Central Terminal.

The bathroom at the Bagel House Diner, located just after you turn left toward the parking area, is generally for customers. There's also a McDonald's Restaurant on NY 22, just before the traffic light in Dover Plains.

Drive time from New York City is 1 hour and 25 minutes.

RIDE DIRECTIONS

0.0 Leaving Dover Plains Railroad Station, turn left onto East Mill Street (which becomes Maple Avenue).

0.8 Turn left onto CR 4/Poplar Hill Road.
The terrain here is quite rural and rolling for 3 miles.

3.9 Turn right onto CR 4/Sinpatch Road.
Just to the right after this turn, note the obelisk. A rally for world peace takes place here annually in the World Peace Sanctuary Park.

5.0 Go straight onto CR 3/Bog Hollow Road.

5.8 Turn left to continue on CR 3/Bog Hollow Road.

7.0 Go straight onto CR 81 into the hamlet of Wassaic.

7.8 The Wassaic General Store appears on the left.
Beyond the store and on the right you'll see the Wassaic train station. The Harlem Valley Rail Trail, a paved recreation trail, will eventually run from the Metro North train station in Wassaic and continue for 46 miles to the town of Chatham in Columbia County, New York. To learn which sections of the trail have been opened, contact the Harlem Valley Rail Trail Association, P.O. Box 356, Millerton, New York 12546, 518-789-9591.

10.8 Turn right onto NY 22 at the stop sign.

11.1 Arrive in Amenia and turn right onto NY 343 east at the traffic light.

11.3 Turn right onto Mechanic Sreet.

11.5 Turn left onto the Harlem Valley Rail Trail.

16.0 Turn left onto CR 58/Coleman Station Road at the intersection with Sheffield Hill Road.
The trail is paved here for 4 miles if you wish to continue cycling into Millerton. Note that the county routes leading into Millerton are very rural here and quite scenic.

16.2 Take the first right onto CR 61/Indian Lake Road.

17.0 At the first left, bear left onto Mill Road.

19.2 Go straight at the intersection with West Street on the left to continue on Mill Road.

19.5 Bear left over the bridge onto unmarked South Center Street.

19.7 Arrive in Millerton and turn right onto US 44/Main Street.
There are a few choices in town for lunch: Taro's on the left on Main Street has an outdoor seating area, as does the Mana Dew Café on the right on Main Street.

19.9 Leaving Millerton, turn right onto CR 62/Maple Avenue (which becomes Sharon Road) at the traffic light.
The Option turns left here.

21.6 Turn right onto CR 61/Indian Lake Road.
The countryside on either side of the road is classic Dutchess County farm country, with rolling terrain, old barns, farmhouses, and some long views.

The residents of a Dutchess County dairy farm

22.2 Bear left at the Y intersection with Downey Road on the right to continue on CR 61/Indian Lake Road.

23.1 Turn left onto Taylor Road at the stop sign at the end of Indian Lake Road.

23.4 Take the first right onto Reagan Road.

24.3 Turn left at the end of Reagan Road onto Sheffield Hill Road.

25.7 Go straight onto CR 1/Sharon Station Road at the stop sign.

27.2 Take the first left to continue on Sharon Station Road.
The route crosses access points to the Harlem Valley Rail Trail.

28.8 Turn left at the end of Sharon Station Road onto NY 343 east.

29.5 Turn right onto CR 2/Leedsville Road.

31.6 Bear right at the Y intersection onto CR 2/South Amenia Road.
Note the stone boundary marker in the little grass triangle in the road. The hamlet of Amenia Union straddles the New York and Connecticut state lines.

35.0 Turn left onto CR 3/Bog Hollow Road.

35.9 Go straight onto CR 4/Poplar Hill Road.

37.0 Bear left to continue on CR 4/Poplar Hill Road.
The route backtracks here; if you missed it earlier, you may note the obelisk in the World Peace Sanctuary Park on the left.

40.0 Turn right at the stop sign onto Maple Avenue (becomes East Mill Street).

40.8 To end the tour, turn right into the Dover Plains train station parking area, just after the railroad tracks.

Option

0.0 From mile 19.9 turn left onto CR 62/Maple Avenue at the traffic light.

1.0 Turn right onto Shagroy Road.
There's a steep uphill here—which, of course, continues downhill. Enjoy the descent, but be careful.

3.0 Shagroy becomes Belgro Road.
Here the route crosses the state line into Litchfield, Connecticut.

3.8 Turn left onto US 44/Millerton Road.

4.5 Turn right onto CT 41 south at the blinking light.
The Riga Mountain Coffee House is 0.5 mile straight through the blinking light.

6.2 Turn right onto CT 112 west at the stop sign.

8.2 Turn left onto US 44 west at the stop sign.

10.0 Arrive in Millerton on US 44/Millerton Road at the traffic light.
Continue from mile 19.9.

New Paltz to Rosendale

- **TOUR DISTANCE:** 30 miles (43 miles with Option)
- **TERRAIN:** Moderate, with rolling terrain. On the Option the rolling terrain has steeper climbs.
- **SPECIAL FEATURES:** New Paltz, Rosendale, Wallkill Valley Rail Trail

This Hudson Valley ride starts in the historic village of New Paltz, from which the route follows country roads leading north through the town of Esopus. The scenery is quite pleasant, with creeks, orchards, and small farms along much of the way.

Starting from the Park and Ride area of the New York Thruway, the directions quickly lead cyclists onto country lanes. There are portable bathrooms at the start and a convenience store just across NY 299. Pleasant back roads lead across a bridge over the Rondout Creek at Eddyville, which was the terminus of the Delaware and Hudson Canal, a 108-mile man-made waterway on which mules pulled barges laden with anthracite coal from northeastern Pennsylvania to Eddyville. Once in Eddyville the coal was off-loaded and sent by barge on the Hudson River to New York City and Canada. William and Maurice Wurtz conceived the idea to build the canal in 1823, when they realized it could provide New York City with a cheap source of energy. Together they created America's first million-dollar private enterprise.

From Eddyville the cycling route parallels the Rondout for 6 miles. There's a wonderful view of the Hudson Valley just before the village of Rosendale. A good lunch spot is the Rosendale Café, which has an outdoor seating area at the rear. The café is located on Main Street and serves original vegetarian cuisine and wonderful desserts. Rosendale sits on a 32-square-mile belt of limestone and is most famous for its natural cement, which was used in the construction of the Brooklyn Bridge, the pedestal of the Statue of Liberty, the Washington Monument, Grand Central Terminal, and thousands of other public works projects.

There's a short climb from Rosendale to a 7-mile section of flat cycling on the Wallkill Valley Rail Trail, which leads back to New Paltz. The trail has a gravel surface and is most suited for hybrid-type bicycles.

The Option on this ride, starting just across the bridge entering New Paltz, is a 13-mile loop that runs west to east over rolling terrain, passing many Hudson Valley fruit orchards. Leave some time at the end of the day to explore Huguenot Street, the site of a collection of early Colonial stone homes that were originally home to a group of French Protestants who fled France to escape religious and political persecution and are today a National Historic Landmark.

DRIVING DIRECTIONS   Take the upper roadway of the George Washington Bridge to the Palisades Parkway north. Leave the parkway at exit 9W (not NY 9W!). Take NY 287/87, the New York State Thruway, north to exit 18, New Paltz. Just beyond the toll-booth turn left into the Park and Ride parking area, following the signs for cars. Park at the rear of the parking area near NY 299.

There is a convenience store with a bathroom just across NY 299. The College Diner is 0.2 mile to the east on NY 299, which can be used for a bathroom stop as well.

Drive time from New York City is 1 hour and 20 minutes.

RIDE DIRECTIONS

0.0 Turn left from the Park and Ride parking area onto the Thruway exit road.

0.1 Bear right onto NY 299 east.
Take care; there's traffic here.

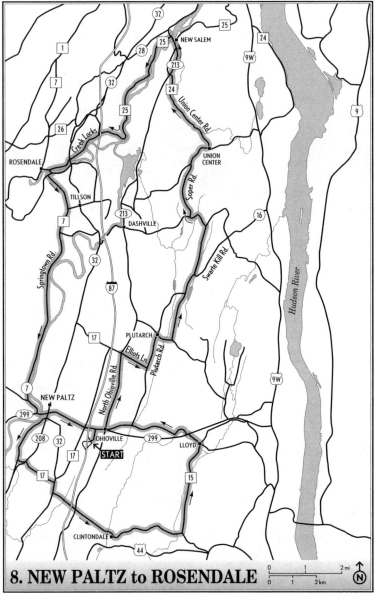

8. NEW PALTZ to ROSENDALE

© The Countryman Press

0.0	Turn left from Park and Ride parking area onto New York Thruway exit road
0.1	Bear Right onto NY 299
0.3	Turn left onto North Ohioville Road
2.4	Turn right onto Elliots Lane
3.3	Turn left onto Plutarch Road (unmarked)
4.2	Turn right onto Blackcreek Road
4.7	Turn left onto North Elting Corners Road
6.1	Go straight onto Swarte Kill Road
6.7	Turn left onto Loughran Lane
8.1	Turn left onto Old Post Road (unmarked)
8.7	Turn right onto Soper Road
10.3	Bear right onto Hardenburgh Road (unmarked)
10.8	Curve right to continue on Hardenburgh Road
11.1	Turn left onto CR 24/Union Center Road
13.7	Turn right onto NY 213
14.8	Turn left onto CR 25/Creek Locks Road
14.9	Bear right to continue on CR 25/Creek Locks Road
15.1	Bear left to continue on CR 25/Creek Locks Road
20.3	Cross NY 32 onto NY 213/Main Street
20.8	Arrive in Rosendale Center and continue on NY 213/Main Street
20.9	Turn left onto CR 7/Keator Avenue
21.1	Bear right uphill
21.2	Bear left onto CR 7/Elting Road at the intersection with Mountain Road
28.0	Turn left onto CR 7/Springtown Road
28.4	Turn left onto NY 299/Main Street and arrive in New Paltz
28.8	Go straight across NY 208 (unmarked) to continue on NY 299/Main Street; Option begins here
30.2	Turn right toward New York Thruway entrance and end tour in Park and Ride parking area

Option (from mile 28.8)

0.0	Turn right onto NY 208/South Chestnut Street (unmarked)
0.1	Turn right onto Mohonk Avenue
0.2	Bear right onto Plains Road (unmarked)
1.6	Turn left onto Cedar Lane
1.8	Go across NY 208 onto Jansen Road
2.9	Turn right onto NY 32
3.2	Turn left onto Brookside Road
3.9	Go straight onto Hurds Road
5.2	Go straight aross CR 22 onto Maple Avenue
5.3	Turn left onto CR 15/Crescent Avenue
7.5	Turn left onto CR 15/Pancake Hollow Road
10.1	Turn left onto CR 12/New Paltz Road
10.7	Turn left onto NY 299
10.8	Turn right immediately onto New Paltz Road (becomes Old Route 299)
13.0	Turn left onto North Ohioville Road Turn right immediately onto NY 299
13.3	Turn left toward New York Thruway entrance and end in Park and Ride parking area

0.3 Take the first left at the traffic light onto North Ohioville Road.

2.4 Turn right onto Elliots Lane at the stop sign.

3.3 At the stop sign turn left at the end of Elliots Lane onto unmarked Plutarch Road.

4.2 Take the first right onto Blackcreek Road at the stop sign.
After crossing the Swarte Kill Creek, you'll see a small, attractive horse farm on the left.

4.7 Take the first left onto North Elting Corners Road.
There's gravel on the road at this turn.

6.1 Go straight onto Swarte Kill Road.

6.7 Turn left onto Loughran Lane.
The signpost for this turn, on the left and on an uphill, is easy to miss. The route itself is uphill here.

8.1 Turn left at the end of Loughran Lane onto unmarked Old Post Road.
Because the road curves, traffic on Old Post Road is difficult to see. Although there's rarely traffic on the route here, it's best to dismount and walk across this turn.

8.7 Take the first right onto Soper Road.

10.3 Bear right onto unmarked Hardenburgh Road at the yield sign.

10.8 With Carney Road on the left, curve right to continue on Hardenburgh Road.

11.1 Turn left at the end of Hardenburgh Road onto CR 24/Union Center Road.

13.7 Turn right onto NY 213 north at the small park.

14.8 Turn left onto CR 25/Creek Locks Road after the bridge across Rondout Creek.
The turn here was the terminus of the D and H Canal Towpath.

14.9 Bear right to continue on CR 25/Creek Locks Road toward Rosendale.

15.1 Bear left at the stop sign to continue on CR 25/Creek Locks Road.

The smiles say it all.

Be careful not to make a hard right here to head steeply uphill. This road parallels Rondout Creek as it continues toward Rosendale and at one point offers a beautiful scenic overlook of the Hudson Valley.

20.3 Cross NY 32 onto NY 213 west/Main Street.
Keep Stewarts convenience store to your right.

20.8 Arrive in Rosendale Center and continue on NY 213/Main Street.
Table Rock Tours and Bicycle Shop is on the right as you enter Rosendale. The Rosendale Café on the right on Main Street is the best bet for lunch.

Leave the Rosendale Café to the right.

20.9 Turn left onto CR 7/Keator Avenue.
You'll climb a steep hill for 0.5 mile, leaving Rosendale.

21.1 Bear right uphill at the church on CR 7/Keator Avenue.

21.2 Bear left uphill on CR 7/Elting Road at the intersection with Mountain Road.

To cycle into New Paltz on the Wallkill Valley Rail Trail, continue onto Mountain Road and turn left immediately onto the trail into New Paltz. Turn left onto NY 299 east/Main Street in New Paltz. You'll see the Green Bridge over the Wallkill River on your right here. Huguenot Street, with its historic stone homes, is also on the right.

28.0 Turn left onto CR 7/Springtown Road at the stop sign.

28.4 Turn left onto NY 299 east/Main Street and cycle across the bridge into New Paltz.
You'll pass Huguenot Street on the left just after crossing the Wallkill River into New Paltz.

28.8 Go straight across unmarked NY 208 at the traffic light to continue on NY 299 east/Main Street.
The Option turns right here. There are three bicycle shops in New Paltz: The Bicycle Depot on Main Street on the left as you enter town, Cycle Path on Main Street beyond The Bicycle Depot, and The Bicycle Rack, which is located to the left on North Front Street.

30.2 Turn right toward the New York Thruway entrance and turn right into the Park and Ride parking area to end the tour.

Option

0.0 From mile 28.8 turn right at the traffic light onto unmarked NY 208/South Chestnut Street.

0.1 Turn right onto Mohonk Avenue.

0.2 Bear right onto unmarked Plains Road.
Don't go uphill!

1.6 Turn left onto Cedar Lane.

1.8 Go across NY 208 onto Jansen Road.
You'll be cycling through fruit orchard country here.

2.9 Turn right at the end of Jansen Road onto NY 32.
Careful! Traffic!

3.2 Take the first left onto Brookside Road.

3.9 Go straight onto Hurds Road at the stop sign.

5.2 Go straight across CR 22 onto Maple Avenue at the stop sign.

5.3 Turn left onto CR 15/Crescent Avenue.

7.5 Turn left at the end of Crescent Avenue onto CR 15/Pancake Hollow Road at the stop sign.

10.1 Turn left at the stop sign at the end of CR 15/Pancake Hollow Road onto CR 12/New Paltz Road.

10.7 Turn left onto NY 299 at the stop sign.

10.8 Turn right immediately onto New Paltz Road (which becomes Old Route 299).

13.0 Turn left onto North Ohioville Road.

Turn right immediately onto NY 299 at the traffic light.
The College Diner is located here.

13.3 Turn left toward the New York Thruway entrance and turn right into the Park and Ride parking area.
Continue straight here to return to the village of New Paltz.

9

New Paltz Day Trip

- **TOUR DISTANCE:** 44 miles
- **TERRAIN:** Easy to moderate, with long gentle sections and some rolling terrain. Any steeper sections are quite short (less than 0.3 mile).
- **SPECIAL FEATURES:** Wallkill Valley Rail Trail, New Paltz Village, historic stone homes on Huguenot Street, Rivendell Winery, the Shawangunk Ridge (the Gunks)

With miles of quiet country roads, mountain bike trails, and rails that have been converted to recreational trails, this Hudson Valley ride provides a superb environment for cycle touring. The surrounding countryside is filled with fruit orchards, rivers flowing into cascades, wineries, and vantage points that provide spectacular views of the Shawangunk Ridge.

This route begins in Orange County in the quaint town of Montgomery, where many of the facades of the historic homes on its main street have recently been renovated. We cross into Ulster County near the town of Wallkill, which is set beside the Wallkill River. Cycling north out of the village of Wallkill, we climb a short hill to discover a commanding view of Hudson Valley and the Shawangunk Mountain Ridge (the Gunks). These mountains have been named by the Nature Conservancy as one of the last fifty great natural places on earth. The Gunks are also favored for their rock climbing, hiking, mountain biking, and parasailing. Here we will also be able to spot the Mohonk Tower, which identifies the location of the Mohonk Mountain House. Built alongside the blue waters of Lake Mohonk in 1869, this grand 251-room hotel is one of America's oldest family-run resorts and has been chosen as one of the five best escapes from New York. Minnewaska State Park is also located in the Gunks, with a preserve that provides miles of carriage and hiking trails and seasonal opportunities for bicycling, scuba diving, swimming, and cross-country skiing.

Multicolored parachutes descend from above as the road passes a parasailing school and then crosses the Wallkill Valley Rail Trail. This rail bed is 12 miles long and stretches from Gardiner to Rosendale. A 5-mile section of the trail can be accessed from this tour and leads directly to Main Street in the village of New Paltz. The surface of the trail is gravel and is most suitable for either hybrid-type or all-terrain bicycles.

New Paltz is home to a campus of the State University of New York and is most famous for Huguenot Street, the site of a collection of early Colonial stone homes that are today a National Historic Landmark. These buildings were originally the homes of a group of French Protestants who fled France because of religious and political persecution.

Leaving New Paltz, we pass the Rivendell Winery, where there's an opportunity to tour or taste the local vintages. Stunning views of the Shawangunk Ridge continue to line the return route to Montgomery.

DRIVING DIRECTIONS   Cross the George Washington Bridge on the upper level and take the Palisades Parkway to exit 18, NY 6 west. Continue around the traffic circle onto NY 6 west toward Central Valley and NY 17 west. Merge onto NY 6/NY 17 west toward Goshen and Monticello. Take exit 124 and turn left at the traffic light toward NY 17A and NY 207 east. Turn right at the traffic light onto NY 207 east. (There's a pit stop here; see below.) Continue through the village of Goshen on NY 207 east. Bear left onto NY 416 and continue to the stop sign at NY 211. Merge right onto NY 211 east into Montgomery. Turn left onto Clinton Street at the Old Fashioned Deli (the sign may be turned so that it seems to read UNION STREET). Turn left at the end of Clinton

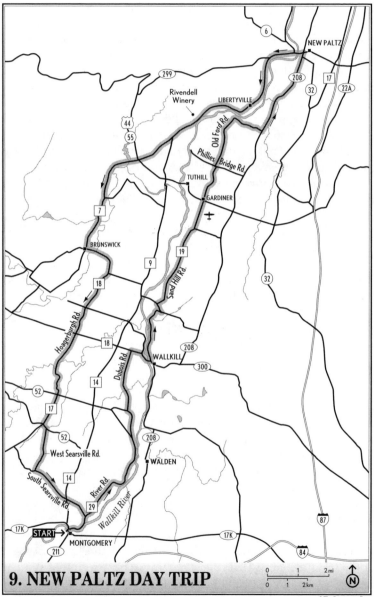

9. NEW PALTZ DAY TRIP

0.0	Turn left from Veterans Park onto Bridge Street
0.2	Merge straight onto NY 17K
0.3	Turn right onto CR 29/River Road (becomes South Montgomery Street)
3.9	Go straight onto NY 52 in Walden (becomes North Montgomery Street)
4.5	Bear right onto Wallkill Road
5.5	Turn right to continue on Wallkill Road
6.4	Go straight onto Dubois Road
7.5	Turn right onto CR 18/Bruyn Turnpike
8.3	Turn left in Wallkill onto River Road
10.3	Turn left onto CR 19/Birch Road
10.6	Turn right onto CR 19/Sand Hill Road
14.1	Pass the airport on the right
14.4	In Gardiner, cross Main Street onto Dusinberre Road
15.6	Turn left onto Phillies Bridge Road
15.7	Turn right immediately onto Old Ford Road
17.8	Turn left onto NY 208
20.8	Arrive in New Paltz and turn right onto NY 299/Main Street
21.1	Leave New Paltz on NY 299 west
22.0	Turn left onto CR 7/Libertyville Road
26.3	Pass Rivendell Winery on the right
28.1	Go straight onto CR 7/Bruynswick Road
31.9	Turn left onto CR 18/Hoagerburgh Road
35.4	Continue straight on Hoagerburgh Road
37.8	Go across NY 52 onto CR 17
38.8	Turn left onto Hill Avenue
39.0	Turn right onto West Searsville Road
40.5	Turn left onto South Searsville Road (unmarked)
41.9	Go straight onto East Searsville Road
42.3	Go straight onto Willow Lane
42.8	Turn right onto CR 29/River Road (unmarked)
43.6	Turn left onto NY 17K
43.7	Go straight onto Bridge Street in Montgomery
43.9	End tour at Veterans Park

Street onto Bridge Street and continue two blocks on Bridge Street to Veterans Park on the right.

For a pit stop on NY 207 east, continue straight at the traffic light for 0.2 mile to either the Burger King or Friendly's restaurants on the left. Return to the traffic light and turn left onto NY 207 east.

Drive time from New York City is 1 hour and 20 minutes.

RIDE DIRECTIONS

0.0 Leaving Veterans Park, turn left onto Bridge Street.

0.2 Merge straight onto NY 17K at the stop sign.

0.3 Turn right onto NY 29/River Road (becomes South Montgomery Street) after crossing the bridge.
The Wallkill River is on the right here beside the road.

3.9 Go straight onto CR 52 (becomes North Montgomery Street) in Walden.

4.5 Bear right onto Walkill Road.

Stopping to sample a local winery's offering

5.5 Turn right to continue on Walkill Road. Rider Road is on the left.

6.4 Go straight onto Dubois Road.
Both sides of the road are lined with apple orchards.

7.5 Turn right at the end of Dubois Road onto CR 18/Bruyn Turnpike.

8.3 Turn left in the town of Walkill onto River Road.
A small deli can be found to the left just after the turn.

10.3 Make a hard left turn at the stop sign onto CR 19/Birch Road.
There's a 0.3-mile climb here to Sand Hill Road.

10.6 Take the first right onto CR 19/Sand Hill Road.
Enjoy the magnificent view of the Shawangunk Mountains (the Gunks) at this turn. Because the route here is located on a ridge overlooking a valley to the west, there are continuing views of the mountains along this road. In the fall foliage season the colors on the side of the Gunks are quite impressive.

14.1 Pass the airport on the right.
On weekends it's fun to take a short break here and watch the multicolored parachutes descending from above.

14.4 Go straight across Main Street in Gardiner onto Dusinberre Road.

15.6 Turn left at the end of Dusinberre Road onto Phillies Bridge Road.
You can also turn right just before Phillies Bridge Road and cycle 5 miles on the Wallkill Valley Rail Trail, which leads directly into New Paltz. Take care not to enter the private drive here instead! The trail's surface is gravel and not suitable for thin tires. Using it enables cyclists to avoid the traffic on NY 208 entering New Paltz. Note, however, that the trail is narrow in spots, and there may be other cyclists, walkers, or joggers using it. As the trail approaches New Paltz it gets much wider. To reach the town center in New Paltz, turn right onto NY 299/Main Street. Huguenot Street, with its historic stone homes, is just to the left as you exit the trail.

15.7 Turn right immediately onto Old Ford Road.

17.8 Turn left at the end of Old Ford Road onto NY 208.
There's fast-moving traffic on this road, but there's also a shoulder.

20.8 Arrive in New Paltz and turn right onto NY 299/Main Street at the traffic light.

You can enjoy a full-service lunch in one of the many restaurants in town or a picnic lunch in Peace Park. To reach the park, turn right onto Plattekill Avenue and continue one block.

21.1 Leave New Paltz on NY 299 west and continue straight until it merges with CR 7.
To visit the stone homes on Huguenot Street, turn right just before the green bridge that crosses the Wallkill River.

22.0 Turn left onto CR 7/Libertyville Road.

26.3 Pass Rivendell Winery on the right.
The winery offers tastings and has an outside deck, which can provide for a pleasant short break. Note that the driveway leading to the winery is loose gravel; walking your bike here is the best choice.

28.1 Go straight on CR 7/Bruynswick Road.

31.9 Turn left onto CR/Hoagerburgh Road.
This is horse farm country, and the big surprise here is the wonderful horse farms that border the route.

35.4 Continue straight on Hoagerburgh Road.

37.8 Go straight across NY 52 onto CR 17.

38.8 Turn left onto Hill Avenue.

39.0 Turn right onto West Searsville Road.

40.5 Turn left at the end of West Searsville Road onto unmarked South Searsville Road.

41.9 Go straight onto East Searsville Road at the stop sign.

42.3 Go straight onto Willow Lane.

42.8 Turn right at the end of Willow Lane onto unmarked CR 29/River Road.

43.6 Turn left at the end of River Road onto NY 17K, cycling across the bridge.

43.7 Go straight onto Bridge Street in Montgomery.

43.9 Arrive at Veterans Park to end the tour.

10

Gunks, Ho!

- **TOUR DISTANCE:** 26 miles (42 miles with Option 1; 52 miles with Options 1 and 2)
- **TERRAIN:** Moderate with rolling terrain throughout
- **SPECIAL FEATURES:** Winding Hills County Park, Montgomery Village

Going from Orange County into Ulster County, this day trip covers an area where the serenity of the surrounding countryside is eventually transformed into stately views of the Hudson Valley's Shawangunk Ridge (the Gunks). The cycling starts in Winding Hills Park just outside the village of Montgomery. Much of the park is set beside a lake, where there are boating and camping as well as numerous hiking and biking trails.

Shortly after leaving the park the ride follows the Wallkill River as it flows toward the Hudson. Small farms line the route as the cycling continues toward lunch in the village of Pine Bush. A 15-mile optional loop (best completed before lunch) leads into the shadows of the Gunks, following rural country lanes with a few short, steep climbs.

The town park in Pine Bush makes for an appealing spot for a picnic lunch. There are also restaurants in the village offering the option of a full-service lunch.

After lunch take the shorter 9-mile return to Winding Hills Park or opt for a ride of 10 miles that loops through the village of Montgomery. This village has recently begun a transformation;

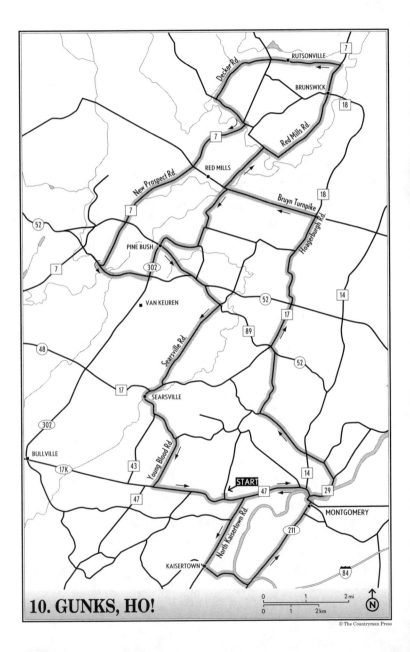

RUTSONVILLE

BRUNSWICK

Decker Rd.

Red Mills Rd.

7

18

7

New Prospect Rd.

RED MILLS

Bruyn Turnpike

18

Hoagerburgh Rd.

52

PINE BUSH

7

302

Searsville Rd.

VAN KEUREN

52

17

89

48

52

17

SEARSVILLE

302

Young Blood Rd.

BULLVILLE

17K

43

START

47

14

29

47

MONTGOMERY

47

211

North Kaisertown Rd.

84

KAISERTOWN

0   1   2 mi

0   1   2 km

10. GUNKS, HO!

N

© The Countryman Press

0.0 Leave Winding Hills Park parking area toward park entrance
1.0 Turn left from Winding Hills Park onto NY 17K (unmarked)
3.2 Bear left onto CR 29/River Road
4.1 Turn left onto Willow Lane
4.5 Go straight onto East Searsville Road
5.0 Go straight onto South Searsville Road
6.4 Turn right onto West Searsville Road
7.8 Turn left onto Hill Avenue (unmarked)
8.0 Turn right onto CR 17
9.0 Go straight onto Fleury Road
10.1 Go straight onto Hoagerburgh Road
11.4 Turn left onto Bruyn Turnpike
12.3 Go straight onto Wallkill Avenue
13.5 Turn left onto Red Mills Road; Option 1 begins here
14.5 Turn right at intersection with Konefal Avenue to continue on Red Mills Road
15.0 Turn right onto North Avenue (becomes Maple Avenue)
16.0 Turn left onto NY 52/Main Street in Pine Bush
17.1 Turn right onto CR 89/Hill Avenue
17.7 Turn right onto Searsville Road
20.0 Turn right onto CR 17 (unmarked)
20.3 Go straight onto CR 43
21.0 Turn left onto Young Blood Road
23.0 Turn left onto NY 17K
24.4 Take the first left at the sign for Winding Hills Park. Option 2 begins here
24.5 Turn left into Winding Hills Park
25.5 End tour at parking area

Option 1 (from mile 13.5)
0.0 Turn right onto Red Mills Road after bridge
1.3 Turn right at intersection with Steen Road to continue on Red Mills Road
3.6 Go straight onto CR 7/Bruynswick Road
4.4 Turn left onto Tillson Lake Road (unmarked)
6.0 Go straight onto Decker Road
7.7 Turn left onto Awosting Road
8.6 Turn right onto CR 7/New Prospect Road
12.3 Go straight onto Pirog Road (becomes Seals Road)
13.5 Turn left onto Ulsterville Road
14.6 Turn left onto NY 302 (unmarked)
15.5 Turn right onto NY 52/Main Street in Pine Bush and continue from mile 16.0

Option 2 (from mile 24.4)
0.0 Go straight on NY 17K
0.6 Turn right onto Kaisertown Road
2.4 Turn left onto East Kaisertown Road (unmarked) at intersection with West Kaisertown Road
3.4 Turn left onto NY 211 (becomes Union Street in Montgomery)
6.2 Turn left onto NY 17K west
8.6 Turn right into Winding Hills Park
9.6 End at parking area

some of the older homes on Clinton Street in the town center are listed on the National Register of Historic Homes and have been renovated. There is a coffee shop on NY 211 at the edge of the village that offers a choice of pastries and desserts.

DRIVING DIRECTIONS   Take the George Washington Bridge to the Palisades Parkway. From the parkway take exit 18, NY 6 west. Continue around the traffic circle onto NY 6 west toward Central Valley and NY 17 west. Merge onto NY 6/NY 17 west toward Goshen and Monticello. Leave NY 6/NY 17 west at exit 124. Turn left at the traffic light toward NY 17A and NY 207 east. Turn right at the next traffic light onto NY 207 east and continue through the village of Goshen on NY 207 east. Bear left onto NY 416 and continue to the stop sign at the intersection with NY 211. Merge right onto NY 211 east into Montgomery. Turn left at the traffic light onto NY 17K west and continue approximately 2 miles. Turn right at the sign for Winding Hills Park and then right into the park at the next sign. Continue straight toward the picnic area and then to the parking area.

There is a bathroom in the parking area.

Drive time from New York City is 1 hour and 20 minutes.

RIDE DIRECTIONS

0.0 Leave the Winding Hills Park parking area toward the park entrance.

1.0 Turn left at the park entrance onto unmarked NY 17K.

3.2 Bear left onto CR 29/River Road.
Turn before reaching the bridge that crosses the Wallkill River. The village of Montgomery is just across the bridge.

4.1 Turn left onto Willow Lane.

4.5 Go straight onto East Searsville Road at the yield sign.

5.0 Go straight onto South Searsville Road at the stop sign.

6.4 Turn right onto West Searsville Road.

7.8 Turn left at the end of West Searsville Road onto unmarked Hill Avenue.

8.0 Take the first right (at the stop sign) onto CR 17.

9.0 Go straight onto Fleury Road at the stop sign.

10.1 Go straight onto Hoagerburgh Road.

11.4 Turn left onto Bruyn Turnpike at the stop sign.
There's an excellent panoramic view of the Shawangunk Ridge at this turn.

12.3 Go straight onto Wallkill Avenue.

13.5 Turn left onto Red Mills Road just before the bridge.
For Option 1, cycle across the bridge and turn right onto Red Mills Road.

14.5 Turn right at the intersection with Konefal Avenue to continue on Red Mills Road.

15.0 At the town park, turn right onto North Avenue (which becomes Maple Avenue in Pine Bush).
If you're planning a picnic lunch, you can shop in Pine Bush and return to the park for your meal.

Breaking for a picnic lunch

16.0 Turn left onto NY 52/Main Street at the traffic light in Pine Bush.
For lunch there are several restaurant choices on Main Street in Pine Bush.

Leave Pine Bush on Main Street/NY 52 east.

17.1 Turn right onto CR 89/Hill Avenue.

17.7 Take the first right onto Searsville Road.

20.0 Turn right at the stop sign at the end of Searsville Road onto unmarked CR 17.

20.3 Go straight onto CR 43 and follow it as it bears to the left.

21.0 Take the first left onto Young Blood Road.

23.0 Turn left onto NY 17K at the stop sign at the end of Youngblood Road.

24.4 Take the first left at the sign for Winding Hills Park.
Option 2 begins here.

24.5 Take the first left into Winding Hills Park.

25.5 End the tour at the Winding Hills Park parking area.

Option 1

0.0 From mile 13.5 turn right onto Red Mills Road after the bridge.
There are orchards and dairy farms lining both sides of the road here.

1.3 Turn right at the intersection with Steen Road to continue on Red Mills Road.

3.6 Go straight onto CR 7/Bruynswick Road at the stop sign.

4.4 Take the first left onto unmarked Tillson Lake Road.
This road has some short but steeper climbs.

6.0 Go straight onto Decker Road.

7.7 Turn left onto Awosting Road.

8.6 Turn right at the stop sign onto CR 7/New Prospect Road.
A general store is located just after this right turn.

12.3 Go straight at the traffic light onto Pirog Road (becomes Seals Road).

13.5 Turn left onto Ulsterville Road.

14.6 Turn left onto unmarked NY 302, returning to Pine Bush.

15.5 Turn right onto NY 52/Main Street at the traffic light in Pine Bush.
Continue from mile 16.0. For a picnic lunch in the town park, return to the traffic light via NY 52/Main Street and turn right onto Maple Avenue.

Option 2

0.0 From mile 24.4 go straight on NY 17K, passing the sign for Winding Hills Park.

0.6 Turn right onto Kaisertown Road.

2.4 Turn left onto unmarked East Kaisertown Road at the intersection with West Kaisertown Road.

3.4 Turn left at the end of East Kaisertown Road onto NY 211 (which becomes Union Street in Montgomery).
Be careful; there's traffic on this road going into Montgomery.

6.2 Turn left onto NY 17K west at the traffic light.
Montgomery has a few cafés where you might stop for a dessert.

8.6 Turn right into Winding Hills Park at the park sign.

9.6 Arrive at the Winding Hills Park parking area.

11

Long Island Berries and Wine

- **TOUR DISTANCE:** 36 miles (40 miles with Option)
- **TERRAIN:** Easy, with mainly flat terrain
- **SPECIAL FEATURES:** Gallucio Family Winery, Wickham's Fruit and Vegetable Farm, New Suffolk Beach

This is an easy ride that follows the flat terrain of eastern Long Island's North Fork, where the scents and sounds of the ocean proliferate throughout the day. The riding traces the shore of Great Peconic Bay, passing town swimming beaches with panoramic seascapes of Long Island's South Fork.

The ride starts in the town of Riverhead, which has a stop on the Long Island Railroad. Riverhead is positioned at the head of Great Peconic Bay, where the north and south forks of Long Island separate to lead toward Orient Point in the north and Montauk Point in the south. The tour follows an easterly course, passing the hamlets of Jamesport and New Suffolk, the home of the first U.S. submarine base. This area is a natural habitat for water birds, and you can often spot Osprey nesting on top of platforms that rise up from the marshlands.

After purchasing a sandwich in Cutchogue, enjoy a picnic lunch on the deck of the Gallucio Family Winery just 0.4 mile from the village center. The winery encourages tasting the local vintages; it's said that these local wines have greatly improved through the years. Another lunch option is Wickham's Farm, located at the village center. It has a picnic table where cyclists can enjoy lunch, and there's always fresh produce on sale at the farm stand. There are even seasonal opportunities to pick your own.

After lunch the pedaling continues onto a causeway that juts out into Little Peconic Bay. Here you can enjoy a swim at New Suffolk Beach. Bridge Lane and Oregon Road lead past the last of Long Island's farmland, and are among the most scenic roads to be found on the North Fork.

DRIVING DIRECTIONS   Take the Long Island Expressway east to exit 71. Continue onto NY 24/CR 94 toward Riverhead. At the traffic circle continue three-quarters around toward NY 25. Turn right immediately after the traffic circle, at the sign reading WEL-COME TO RIVERHEAD. This is the public parking area for the town of Riverhead. Park toward the rear, alongside the water.

There are bathrooms at the gas station on the right as you drive around the traffic circle.

The Long Island Railroad departs from Penn Station in New York and Jamaica Station in Queens and stops in Riverhead.

Drive time from New York City is 1 hour and 40 minutes.

RIDE DIRECTIONS

0.0 Leave the rear of the parking area on unmarked McDermott Avenue at Heirloom Country Collectibles.

0.1 Turn right onto East Main Street at the traffic light.

0.8 Turn right onto Hubbard Avenue.

2.5 Turn right across the tracks to continue on Hubbard Avenue/Meeting House Creek Road.

3.0 Turn left onto Peconic Bay Boulevard.

9.1 Turn left onto Bay Avenue.
There's a beach here on the right with views across Great Peconic Bay to the South Fork of Long Island.

9.7 Turn right onto NY 25 at the Hess gas station.

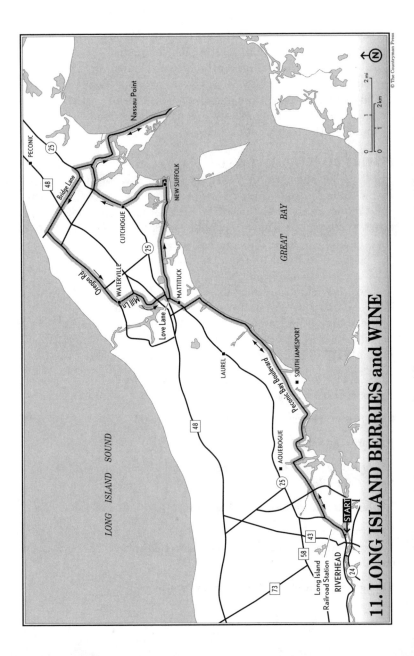

11. LONG ISLAND BERRIES and WINE

LONG ISLAND SOUND

GREAT BAY

PECONIC

48

Bridge Lane

Nassau Point

25

Oregon Rd

NEW SUFFOLK

CUTCHOGUE

25

WATERVILLE

Mill Ln

Love Lane

MATTITUCK

LAUREL

48

Peconic Bay Boulevard

SOUTH JAMESPORT

AQUEBOGUE

25

43

58

73

Long Island Railroad Station

RIVERHEAD

START

24

© The Countryman Press

N

2 mi

2 km

0.0 Leave from rear of parking area on McDermott Avenue (unmarked) in Riverhead
0.1 Turn right onto East Main Street
0.8 Turn right onto Hubbard Avenue
2.5 Turn right to continue on Hubbard Avenue/Meeting House Creek Road
3.0 Turn left onto Peconic Bay Boulevard
9.1 Turn left onto Bay Avenue
9.7 Turn right onto NY 25
9.9 Turn right onto New Suffolk Avenue (becomes Main Street)
13.2 Turn left onto First Street in New Suffolk
13.4 Turn left onto Orchard Street
13.6 Turn right onto Fifth Street
15.1 Arrive in Cutchogue Village
15.2 Turn right onto NY 25; pass Wickham's Fruit Farm on the right
15.9 Turn right onto Eugene Road
16.3 Turn right onto Skunk Lane/Bay Avenue
17.3 Bear right toward beach
17.5 Arrive at Cutchogue/New Suffolk Beach; Option for 4-mile round-trip ride to Nassau Point
Reverse direction to leave beach on Bay Avenue
18.9 Bear right as Bay Avenue becomes Skunk Lane
19.2 Turn left onto NY 25
19.4 Turn right onto Bridge Lane
20.4 Cross CR 48 to continue on Bridge Lane
21.2 Turn left onto Oregon Road
23.8 Turn left onto Mill Lane
24.3 Turn right onto Wickham Avenue
Bear left immediately at Y intersection
24.9 Turn left at end of Wickham Avenue onto Grand Avenue
25.4 Go straight across CR 48 to continue on Grand Avenue
25.6 Turn right onto NY 25
25.7 Bear left at intersection with Love Lane to continue on NY 25
26.0 Turn left onto Bay Avenue
26.6 Turn right onto Peconic Bay Boulevard
32.8 Turn right onto Meeting House Creek Road/Hubbard Avenue
33.2 Turn left onto Hubbard Avenue after railroad tracks
35.0 Turn left onto East Main Street
35.7 Turn left onto McDermott Avenue and end tour at parking area
36.0 Arrive at parking area to end the tour

Enjoying the excellent local vintages

9.9 Turn right onto New Suffolk Avenue (becomes Main Street in New Suffolk).
The route is very scenic here, passing waterfront homes and wetlands on Great Peconic Bay.

13.2 Turn left at the end of Main Street onto First Street in New Suffolk.
This hamlet is signposted as the home of the first U.S. submarine base.

13.4 Turn left at the end of First Street onto Orchard Street.

13.6 Turn right at the end of Orchard Street onto Fifth Street.

15.1 Arrive in Cutchogue Village.
There's a deli on the left at the traffic light.

15.2 Turn right at the traffic light onto NY 25.
You'll pass Wickham's Fruit Farm on the right. The farm has a picnic table and sells freshly picked produce, or you can often pick it yourself. If you turn left at the traffic

light here and travel 0.4 mile, you'll reach the Gallucio Family Winery. Here you can picnic on the deck and enjoy tasting the locally produced wines.

Turn right onto NY 25 east to leave Wickham's Fruit Farm.

15.9 Turn right at the traffic light onto Eugene Road.

16.3 Turn right at the stop sign at the end of Eugene Road onto Skunk Lane/Bay Avenue.

17.3 Bear right toward the beach.

17.5 Arrive at Cutchogue/New Suffolk Beach.
This beach offers the opportunity for a swim and has bathrooms where you can change. You can also continue to Nassau Point at the end of the road for a 4-mile out and back. Here there's a pleasant view across the bay. To leave the beach, reverse direction.

18.9 Bear right as Bay Avenue becomes Skunk Lane.

19.2 Turn left at the stop sign at the end of Skunk Lane onto NY 25.

19.4 Turn right onto Bridge Lane.

20.4 Go straight across CR 48 to continue on Bridge Lane.
The next 3 miles are among the most scenic that remain on the North Fork.

21.2 Turn left onto Oregon Road.

23.8 Turn left onto Mill Lane.

24.3 Turn right onto Wickham Avenue at the stop sign.

Bear left immediately at the Y intersection.

24.9 Turn left at the end of Wickham Avenue onto Grand Avenue.
There are two Grand Avenues here. Turn left at the second one.

25.4 Go straight across CR 48 at the traffic light to continue on Grand Avenue.

25.6 Turn right at the stop sign at the end of Grand Avenue onto NY 25 west.

25.7 Bear left at the intersection with Love Lane to continue on NY 25 west.

26.0 Turn left onto Bay Avenue at the Hess gas station.

26.6 Turn right onto Peconic Bay Boulevard.
Mattituck's Beach on Peconic Bay is on the left.

32.8 Turn right onto Meeting House Creek Road/Hubbard Avenue.

33.2 Turn left onto Hubbard Avenue after the railroad tracks.

35.0 Turn left onto East Main Street at the stop sign.

35.7 Turn left onto McDermott Avenue.

36.0 Arrive at the parking area to end the tour.

12

Shelter Island

- **TOUR DISTANCE:** 27 miles (42 miles with Option 1; 60 miles with Option 2)
- **TERRAIN:** Easy to moderate
- **SPECIAL FEATURES:** Town of Greenport, town of Sag Harbor

The Manhanset Indians gave Shelter Island its name—an island sheltered by islands—before the arrival of the first English settlers in 1652. This island jewel is neatly tucked away in Peconic Bay between Long Island's North Fork and South Fork. Nearly one third of this 8,000-acre island is owned by the Nature Conservancy and is kept in a forever-wild state. Ferry service from the mainland runs regularly from either the town of Greenport on the north, or Sag Harbor on the south. There is also an auto ferry that connects from Orient Point, the most easterly location on the North Fork, to New London, Connecticut.

The tour begins on the island at the north ferry parking area in Greenport, which is also the last stop on the Long Island Railroad North Fork line. The Bike Stop Cycling Shop at 200 Front Street in Greenport rents bicycles and is just a few minutes' walk from the ferry parking area. A 10-minute ferry crossing lands at the town of Dering Harbor, a busy seasonal village with quite a few shops and restaurants. The ride leads to Crescent Beach, where a swim is always a pleasant interlude and where lunch can be enjoyed in a restaurant with an outdoor deck overlooking the beach. The beach also has bathrooms for changing.

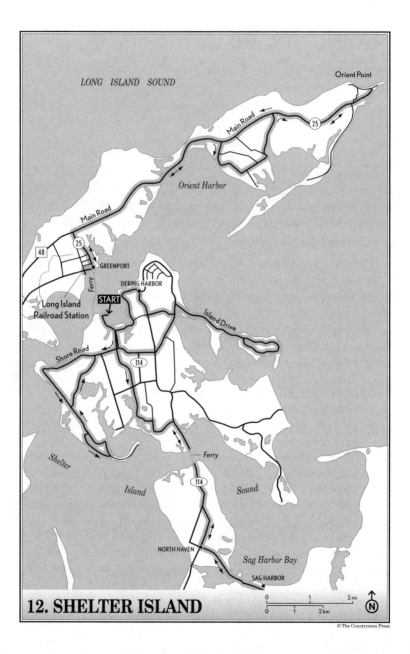

LONG ISLAND SOUND

Orient Point

Main Road

25

Orient Harbor

Main Road

48   25

GREENPORT

Ferry

DERING HARBOR

START

Island Drive

Long Island
Railroad Station

Shore Road

114

Shelter

Island

Ferry

114

Sound

Sag Harbor Bay

NORTH HAVEN

SAG HARBOR

0   1   2 mi

0   1   2 km

N

12. SHELTER ISLAND

© The Countryman Press

```
 0.0  Leave north ferry on Shelter Island via NY 114
 0.3  Turn left on NY 114/Chase Avenue in Dering Harbor (becomes North Ferry Road)
 0.9  Turn right onto West Neck Road (becomes Shore Road)
 2.5  Turn left at Crescent Beach to continue on Shore Road
 3.2  Bear left uphill (becomes Rocky Point Road)
 3.4  Turn left onto Nostrand Parkway
 4.4  Go straight across West Neck Road onto Brander Parkway
 5.1  Turn right onto Petticoat Lane
 5.2  Turn left onto Peconic Avenue
 5.8  Go straight onto unmarked East Brander Parkway (becomes North Brander Parkway)
 6.7  Go straight onto Brander Parkway
 7.7  Turn right onto West Neck Road
 8.7  Turn left onto CR 42/West Neck Road
 9.0  Turn right onto NY 114/North Ferry Road; Option 1 begins here
10.1  Go straight onto Manwaring Road toward Ram Island as NY 114 continues right
10.5  Turn left onto Ram Island Road
11.6  Turn right onto Ram Island Drive
13.2  Continue straight onto North Ram Island Drive
14.1  Turn right onto South Ram Island Drive
14.9  Turn left onto Ram Island Drive
16.7  Turn left onto Ram Island Road
16.9  Turn right onto Corbetts Lane
17.5  Turn right onto Manhanset Road
      Bear right along shore and merge straight onto Winthrop Road (unmarked)
19.4  Turn left onto NY 114/North Ferry Road
20.0  Turn right onto CR 42/West Neck Road (becomes Shore Road)
21.4  Turn left onto Shore Road at Crescent Beach
22.1  Bear left uphill on Shore Road (becomes Rocky Point Road)
22.3  Turn left onto Nostrand Parkway
23.3  Turn left onto West Neck Road
24.3  Turn right onto CR 42/West Neck Rd
25.6  Turn left onto NY 114 toward north ferry
26.8  End tour at north ferry; Option 2 begins here


      Option 1(from mile 9.0)
 0.0  Turn right onto North Midway Road (becomes South Midway Road)
 2.6  Turn right to continue on South Midway Road
 3.9  Turn right onto NY 114 south
 4.6  Arrive at south ferry to Sag Harbor
      Leave south ferry straight onto NY 114 south
 6.4  Turn left to continue on NY 114 toward Sag Harbor
 7.6  Arrive in Sag Harbor
      Leave Sag Harbor via NY 114 north toward south ferry
 8.8  Turn right to continue on NY 114
10.6  Arrive at south ferry
      Leave south ferry straight onto NY 114 north
11.3  Turn left onto South Midway Road
12.6  Turn left to continue on South Midway Road (becomes North Midway Road)
15.2  Turn right onto West Neck Road and continue from mile 9.0


      Option 2 (from mile 26.8)
 0.0  Take north ferry to Greenport
      Leave ferry bearing right onto Third Street
 0.1  Turn right onto Front Street
 1.0  Turn left onto NY 25/Main Street
 1.8  Turn right onto NY 25/Main Road/Orient Road
 4.9  Turn right onto Village Lane into Orient Business District
 5.5  Turn left onto King Street
 6.0  Turn left onto Narrow River Road
 7.6  Turn right onto NY 25
 9.7  Arrive at Orient Point
      Reverse direction to leave Orient Point on NY 25 toward Greenport
17.0  Turn left in Greenport to continue on NY 25
17.8  Turn right onto Front Street
18.0  Turn left onto Third Street
18.1  End at ferry to Shelter Island
```

The island's quiet lanes are constantly revealing changing views of Peconic Bay. The pedaling eventually leads to a causeway on a remote section where there are panoramic views of the bay on either side of the road and opportunities to see ospreys nesting atop platforms. The Ram's Head Inn, located on this part of the island, offers an outdoor dining area overlooking Dering Harbor

Enjoying the ferry transfer to the island

and is a wonderfully romantic lunch stop.

To explore Long Island's South Fork, take the short ferry hop to Sag Harbor. This waterside community is a busy resort area for the Hamptons crowd during the summer.

The tour ends with a ferry ride back to the village of Greenport, which is a town worth exploring. On the tour a flat, 18-mile optional loop leads to Orient Point at the easternmost tip of Long Island's North Fork. This loop passes through the quaint village of Orient-by-the-Sea, where there is a general store that sells cold drinks.

DRIVING DIRECTIONS   Take the Long Island Expressway to the end, exit 73. Continue onto CR 58 east toward Greenport and Orient. Continue straight onto NY 25 east, following it to the town of Greenport. As you enter Greenport, turn right and then left, following the signs to the Shelter Island Ferry. At the ferry you may park in the parking area adjacent to the north ferry terminal. This ride starts and finishes at the terminus of the Long Island Railroad's Greenport Train Station.

There is a bathroom near the ferry terminal.

Drive time from New York City is 2 hours and 15 minutes.

RIDE DIRECTIONS

0.0 Leave the north ferry on Shelter Island via NY 114 south.

0.3 Turn left onto NY 114 south/Chase Avenue (becomes North Ferry Road) in Dering Harbor.
The village of Dering Harbor has shopping and restaurants.

0.9 Turn right onto West Neck Road (becomes Shore Road).

2.5 Turn left at Crescent Beach to continue on Shore Road.
Crescent Beach offers an opportunity for lunch and a swim; there are both seasonal restaurants and places to change. If you don't choose the Option leading to Sag Harbor, the route loops back here at mile 21.4.

3.2 Bear left uphill on Shore Road (becomes Rocky Point Road).
The road leaves the beach and climbs for about 0.3 mile.

3.4 Turn left onto Nostrand Parkway.

4.4 Go straight across West Neck Road onto Brander Parkway.

5.1 Turn right onto Petticoat Lane.

5.2 Take the first left onto Peconic Avenue.
The road here passes a small community of waterfront homes and offers pleasant views of Peconic Bay.

5.8 Go straight onto unmarked East Brander Parkway (becomes North Brander Parkway).
Follow the road as it loops back upon itself.

6.7 Go straight onto Brander Parkway at the white flagpole.

7.7 Turn right onto West Neck Road.

8.7 Turn right onto CR 42/West Neck Road.

9.0 Turn right onto NY 114 south/North Ferry Road.
The Option to the south ferry and Sag Harbor turns right onto North Midway Road just before NY 114 south.

10.1 Go straight onto Manwaring Road toward Ram Island as NY 114 south continues right.

10.5 Turn left onto Ram Island Road at the circle.

11.6 Turn right onto Ram Island Drive.
The ride here follows a narrow causeway with panoramic views of the bay on both sides of the road. Look for osprey nests atop the poles beside the road.

13.2 Continue straight onto North Ram Island Drive at the Ram's Head Inn.
The road's surface on Ram Island is bumpy. The route makes a 2.7-mile loop back to the intersection with the Ram's Head Inn.

14.1 Turn right onto South Ram Island Drive.

14.9 Turn left onto Ram Island Drive at the Ram's Head Inn.
This is a wonderful spot for lunch. The inn has an outdoor dining area at the rear that overlooks Dering Harbor.

16.7 Turn left onto Ram Island Road.

16.9 Turn right onto Corbetts Lane.

17.5 Turn right onto Manhanset Road toward the town of Dering Harbor.

Bear right at the thru traffic sign and merge straight onto unmarked Winthrop Road.
There is a spectacular community of waterfront homes here that overlooks the bay toward the village of Dering Harbor.

19.4 Turn left onto NY 114/North Ferry Road.

20.0 Turn right onto CR 42/West Neck Road (which becomes Shore Road).

21.4 Turn left onto Shore Road at Crescent Beach.
Here's the second opportunity for lunch and a swim. Note that the restaurant here is seasonal.

22.3 Bear left uphill on Shore Road (which becomes Rocky Point Road).

22.5 Turn left onto Nostrand Parkway.

23.3 Turn left onto West Neck Road.

24.3 Turn right onto CR 42/West Neck Road.

25.6 Turn left onto NY 114 toward the north ferry.

26.8 Arrive at the north ferry to end the tour.
Option 2 begins here.

Option 1

0.0 From mile 9.0 turn right onto North Midway Road (which becomes South Midway Road).

2.6 Turn right to continue on South Midway Road.

3.9 Turn right onto NY 114 south.

4.6 Arrive at the south ferry to Sag Harbor.
After a short ferry hop, NY 114 south continues on the South Fork.

Leave the south ferry straight onto NY 114 south.

6.4 Turn left at the traffic light to continue on NY 114 south toward Sag Harbor.

7.6 Arrive in Sag Harbor.
This is a busy summer resort community with a choice of good restaurants that overlook the water.

Leave Sag Harbor by reversing direction, returning to the ferry on NY 114 north.

8.8 Turn right to continue on NY 114 north toward the south ferry.

10.6 Arrive at the south ferry.
Once back on Shelter Island, leave the ferry on NY 114 north.

11.3 Turn left onto South Midway Road.

12.6 Turn left to continue on South Midway Road (which becomes North Midway Road).

15.2 Turn right onto West Neck Road.
Continue from mile 9.0.

Option 2

0.0 From mile 26.8 take the north ferry to Greenport.

Leave the ferry, bearing right onto Third Street in Greenport.
Greenport is a small town that is definitely worth exploring. It boasts a large water-side dock, many interesting shops, good dessert and ice cream shops, and a bicycle shop.

0.1 Turn right at the traffic light onto Front Street.

1.0 Turn left onto NY 25 east/Main Street.

1.8 Turn right onto NY 25/Main Road/Orient Road.

4.9 Turn right onto Village Lane toward the Orient Business District.
Orient is a quaint, waterside hamlet that has a general store.

5.5 Turn left onto King Street.

6.0 Turn left onto Narrow River Road.

7.6 Turn right onto NY 25 east toward Orient Point.
Taking a left here will shorten the ride by 5 miles.

9.7 Arrive at Orient Point.
This is the most easterly point on Long Island's North Fork. There's a year-round ferry service here connecting Long Island with New London, Connecticut.

Return to Greenport from Orient Point on NY 25 west.

17.0 Turn left in Greenport to continue on NY 25 west.

17.8 Turn right onto Front Street toward the Shelter Island ferry.

18.0 Turn left onto Third Street at the traffic light.

18.1 Arrive at the Shelter Island ferry.

NEW JERSEY

13

Andover to Hope

- **TOUR DISTANCE:** 40 miles (46 miles with Option)
- **TERRAIN:** Moderate, with rolling terrain
- **SPECIAL FEATURES:** Hope Village, Kittatinny State Park and Airport, Andover Village

Located at the top of northwestern New Jersey, Sussex and Warren Counties are truly a cyclist's delight. This pristine area is a unique combination of rural beauty with a country setting that includes beautiful foliage and wooded spots, picturesque farms, and numerous lakes and ponds.

This ride starts in a park with a lakeside setting and leads through miles of lightly traveled country roads. As we cross the county line from Sussex to Warren, we pass Johnsonburg Village in Frelinghuysen Township, with its old wood frame buildings and general store lining the main street. The route continues in a westerly direction and is bordered by meadows, ponds, and working farms. Jenny Jump Mountain to the south signals our arrival in Hope Village. The historic hamlet of Hope, founded in 1769 by Moravian settlers, is listed on the National Register of Historic Places. In another time grain from the gristmill in Hope was hauled over Jenny Jump Mountain. Lunch at the Village Café is pleasing whether indoors or at the tranquil outdoor streamside setting. Just across the road from the Village Café is the Inn at Mill Race Pond, whose main building was a gristmill from 1770 to the 1950s.

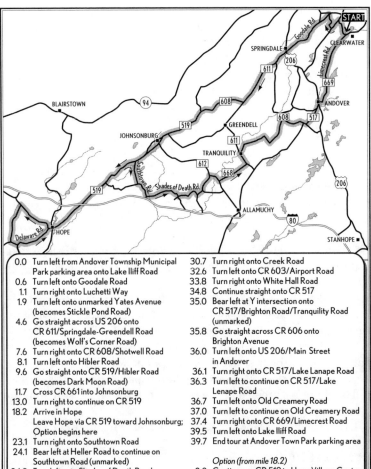

0.0	Turn left from Andover Township Municipal Park parking area onto Lake Iliff Road
0.6	Turn left onto Goodale Road
1.1	Turn right onto Luchetti Way
1.9	Turn left onto unmarked Yates Avenue (becomes Stickle Pond Road)
4.6	Go straight across US 206 onto CR 611/Springdale-Greendell Road (becomes Wolf's Corner Road)
7.6	Turn left onto CR 608/Shotwell Road
8.1	Turn left onto Hibler Road
9.6	Go straight onto CR 519/Hibler Road (becomes Dark Moon Road)
11.7	Cross CR 661 into Johnsonburg
13.0	Turn right to continue on CR 519
18.2	Arrive in Hope Leave Hope via CR 519 toward Johnsonburg; Option begins here
23.1	Turn right onto Southtown Road
24.1	Bear left at Heller Road to continue on Southtown Road (unmarked)
24.9	Turn left onto Shades of Death Road (unmarked)
27.5	Turn left at Y intersection onto Long Bridge Road (unmarked)
27.7	Turn left onto Quaker Church Road
28.6	Turn right onto CR 612/Johnsonburg Road
29.1	Turn left onto CR 668/Cemetery Road/Maple Lane
30.2	Turn left onto CR 611/Kennedy Road

30.7	Turn right onto Creek Road
32.6	Turn left onto CR 603/Airport Road
33.8	Turn right onto White Hall Road
34.8	Continue straight onto CR 517
35.0	Bear left at Y intersection onto CR 517/Brighton Road/Tranquility Road (unmarked)
35.8	Go straight across CR 606 onto Brighton Avenue
36.0	Turn left onto US 206/Main Street in Andover
36.1	Turn right onto CR 517/Lake Lanape Road
36.3	Turn left to continue on CR 517/Lake Lenape Road
36.7	Turn left onto Old Creamery Road
37.0	Turn left to continue on Old Creamery Road
37.4	Turn right onto CR 669/Limecrest Road
39.5	Turn left onto Lake Iliff Road
39.7	End tour at Andover Town Park parking area

Option (from mile 18.2)

0.0	Continue on CR 519 to Hope Village Center
0.1	Continue straight through Hope Village onto CR 609
0.2	Turn right onto CR 655/Cedar Street/Mt. Herman Road
1.9	Turn left onto South Locust Lake Road
3.6	Turn left onto CR 609/Delaware Road
5.9	Arrive in Hope Village and continue straight onto CR 519; continue from mile 18.2

13. ANDOVER to HOPE

0 1 2 mi
0 1 2 km

N

© The Countryman Press

A 6-mile option continues in a westerly direction toward Mt. Hermon and the Delaware Water Gap. This route, hillier than the regular tour, leads back to Hope Village. The return to Andover is marked by terrain that is gentler, with some miles of flat cycling on Shades of Death Road. If you look at a local map you can find other similarly "dark" names, such as Dark Moon Road and Ghost Lake. Because of these we've often had fun offering this tour as our Halloween ride, with paste-on images of ghosts, goblins, and jack-o'-lanterns appearing on our cue sheets and maps.

The ride through Andover Village offers opportunities to browse in some of the antiques shops. Just before the end of the tour, the route passes Kittatinny State Park and Airport, providing a restful lakeside interlude during which you can view small planes taking off and landing.

DRIVING DIRECTIONS   From the George Washington Bridge take I-80 west approximately 45 miles to exit 27B. Continue onto NJ 183 north in Netcong. Continue halfway around the traffic circle and bear right onto NJ 183/US 206 north through Netcong. After 1.5 miles continue onto US 206 north for 5.5 miles through Andover. Turn right onto CR 669/Limecrest Road north for 2.7 miles. Turn left onto Lake Iliff Road, just past the Andover Municipal Firehouse Building. Take the first left at the low stone wall into the lower parking area of Andover Township Municipal Park.

There are bathrooms in the park at the top of the stairs on the right.

Drive time from New York City is 1 hour and 15 minutes.

RIDE DIRECTIONS

0.0 Turn left from Andover Township Municipal Park onto Lake Iliff Road.

0.6 Turn left onto Goodale Road.

1.1 Turn right onto Luchetti Way.
Take care on this road; it's narrow, and it twists as it climbs and descends.

1.9 Turn left at the end of Luchetti Way onto unmarked Yates Avenue (which becomes Stickle Pond Road).

4.6 At the traffic light go straight across US 206 south onto CR 611/Springdale-Greendell Road (which becomes Wolf's Corner Road). *The ride now traces the borders of the Whittingham Wildlife Management Area.*

7.6 Turn right onto CR 608 west/Shotwell Road.

8.1 Turn left onto Hibler Road. *Look for the octagonal-sided house on the left 0.5 mile before crossing CR 661. CR 519 is also named Dark Moon Road on some local maps.*

9.6 Go straight onto NJ 519/Hibler Road (becomes Dark Moon Road).

11.7 Go straight across CR 661 into Johnsonburg. *There's a general store on the left.*

13.0 Turn right to continue on CR 519 south. *Note the tower on top of Jenny Jump Mountain on the left about a mile before entering Hope.*

18.2 Arrive in Hope Village. *The Village Café is the best bet for lunch, with both indoor full-service meals and outdoor take-out service. The Option starts and finishes here.*

Leave Hope by reversing direction, following CR 519 north to Johnsonburg.

23.1 Turn right onto Southtown Road.

24.1 Take the first left at the intersection with Heller Road on the right to continue on unmarked Southtown Road.

24.9 Turn left at the end of Southtown Road onto unmarked Shades of Death Road. *Enjoy the cycling on this flat and very scenic section of the route.*

27.5 Turn left at the Y intersection onto unmarked Long Bridge Road.

27.7 Take the first left onto Quaker Church Road.

28.6 Turn right at the end of Quaker Church Road onto CR 612 south/Johnsonburg Road.

29.1 Take the first left onto CR 668 north/Cemetery Road/Maple Lane

The brush and woods along this New Jersey country lane seem soft and quiet after dropping their autumn leaves.

30.2 Turn left at the end of CR 668/Cemetery Road/Maple Lane onto CR 611 north/Kennedy Road.

30.7 Turn right onto Creek Road.

32.6 Turn left at the end of Creek Road onto CR 603 north/Airport Road.

33.8 Turn right onto White Hall Road before reaching the tunnel.

34.8 Continue straight onto CR 517.

35.0 Bear left at the Y intersection onto unmarked CR 517/Brighton Road/Tranquility Road.

35.8 Go straight across CR 606 onto Brighton Avenue at the traffic light.

36.0 Turn left onto US 206/Main Street in Andover.
If time allows and you are so inclined, enjoy browsing the antiques shops in Andover.

36.1 Take the first right at the traffic light onto CR 517 north/Lake Lanape Road.

36.3 Turn left at the stop sign to continue on CR 517 north/Lake Lenape Road.

36.7 Turn left onto Old Creamery Road before the uphill.

37.0 Turn left to continue on Old Creamery Road.

37.4 Turn right at the end of Old Creamery Road onto CR 669 north/Limecrest Road.
Here the ride passes the Kittatinny State Park and Airport. On weekends there's a great deal of airport activity, with many small vintage planes taking off and landing.

39.5 Turn left onto Lake Iliff Road.

39.7 Turn left into Andover Township Municipal Park to end the tour.

Option

0.0 From mile 18.2 continue on CR 519 through the blinking light in Hope Village Center.
There's a short, steep climb from the Village Café to the traffic light in the center of Hope.

0.1 Continue straight through Hope Village onto CR 609.

0.2 Turn right onto CR 655 north/Cedar Street/Mt. Herman Road.

1.9 Turn left onto South Locust Lake Road.

3.6 Turn left at the end of South Locust Lake Road onto CR 609 east/Delaware Road toward Hope Village.

5.9 Arrive in Hope Village and continue straight through the blinking light onto CR 519.
Continue from mile 18.2.

14

New Jersey's Great Northwest

- **TOUR DISTANCE:** 44 miles (51 miles with Option)
- **TERRAIN:** Moderate, with a few short but steeper climbs
- **SPECIAL FEATURES:** Blairstown Airport, Andover Village

Beginning from Blairstown Airport, this route leads north into Sussex County. The remote Delaware Water Gap Recreational Area follows the western border of this ride, which then continues over lightly traveled roads, passing horse farms and dense woodlands. At the beginning of the ride it's possible to cycle on a 2.2-mile section of the unpaved Paulins Kill Valley Trail. This trail follows the abandoned New York, Susquehanna and Western Railroad's right-of-way for 27 miles between Sparta Junction in Sussex County and Hainesburg and Columbia in Warren County.

The terrain and landscape on the tour become rolling just after Blairstown Center. At 8.2 miles, the route crosses from Warren to Sussex County and then continues straight onto Fredon-Greendell Road, passing Water Mill Farm. The scene here is picture postcard perfect, the image of Currier and Ives. It's worth stopping a few hundred yards beyond, at the top of a small rise, to look back over this pastoral world and take a photo or two if you have a camera with you.

The ride passes the Whittingham Wildlife Management Area on the way to Andover Village. You'll find that there's some traffic on US 206 for about 2 miles, but there's also a wide shoulder here. The 6-mile scenic Option loops out and around, passing Lake Iliff before rejoining the main tour. A good choice for lunch is the Andover Diner on the right as you enter the village. For those who enjoy antiquing, there are opportunities to browse the antiques shops in the village before setting out on the afternoon loop.

After lunch the route becomes quite gentle for 12 miles, or about one half of the afternoon's ride. The scenery is quite pleasant, with many panoramic views of meadows and farms on either side of the road. From Southtown Road the cycling once again leads through dense woodlands and rolling terrain. Just before your arrival at Blairstown Airport there are remarkable views of the mountains and the Delaware Water Gap from a vantage point on Dry Road. If there's time, a pause at Blairstown Airport at the completion of the ride can be delightful. On weekends the airport is very active, with many biplanes, vintage World War II aircraft, and glider planes taking off and landing. If the café at the airport is open, order the homemade apple pie.

DRIVING DIRECTIONS   Take the George Washington Bridge to I-80 west to exit 12, Hope. Turn right at the end of the exit ramp onto CR 521 north toward Blairstown. Continue 4.8 miles and turn left at the end of CR 521 onto CR 521/NJ 94. Turn left after 0.2 mile onto CR 616/Cedar Lake Road and continue 2.2 miles. Turn right onto Airport Road and immediately cross Lambert Road, continuing into the parking area of Blairstown Airport.

There is a restaurant with a bathroom at the airport.

Drive time from New York City is 1 hour and 20 minutes.

RIDE DIRECTIONS

0.0 Leave the Blairstown Airport parking area on Airport Road.

0.1 Go straight across Lambert Road on Airport Road.
Take care to cross Lambert Road and not to turn left onto Lambert Road. The unpaved Paulins Kill Valley Trail is to the left of Lambert Road. It's possible to access this trail by turning left onto Lambert Road for 0.2 mile, then turning right onto the trail itself. Riders can cycle on the trail for 2.2 miles to reach Blairstown.

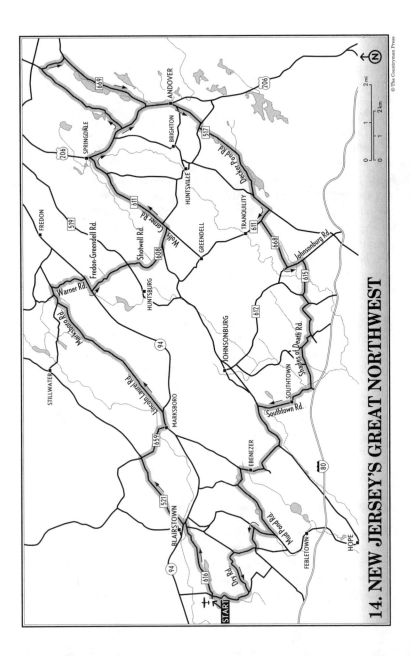

14. NEW JERSEY'S GREAT NORTHWEST

0.0 Leave Blairstown Airport parking area on Airport Road
0.1 Go straight across Lambert Road
0.2 Turn left onto CR 616/Cedar Lake Road
2.3 Turn left onto CR 521/NJ 94
2.5 Turn right onto CR 521/Stillwater Road
4.7 Turn right onto CR 659/Spring Valley Road
6.0 Turn left onto NJ 94
6.3 Turn left onto Lincoln Laurel Road
8.2 Go straight onto Fredon Road (becomes Marksboro Road)
11.4 Turn right onto Warner Road
12.4 Turn right onto NJ 94
12.9 Turn left onto Fredon-Greendell Road
14.2 Go straight across CR 519 onto CR 608/Shotwell Road
16.1 Turn left onto CR 611/Wolfs Corner Road (becomes Springdale-Greendell Road)
19.1 Turn right onto US 206
20.3 *Option begins here*
21.4 Arrive in Andover and continue on US 206
21.9 Turn right onto CR517/Brighton Road/Tranquility Road (becomes Decker Pond Road)
23.1 Turn left to continue on CR 517
26.2 Turn right onto CR 611
26.6 Turn left onto CR 668/Maple Lane/Cemetery Road
28.0 Turn left onto CR 612/Johnsonburg Road
28.5 Turn right onto CR 615/Long Bridge Road
29.4 Go straight to continue on Long Bridge Road at intersection with Quaker Church Road
29.7 Turn right onto Shades of Death Road
30.8 Bear right to continue on Shades of Death Road (unmarked)
32.3 Turn right onto Southtown Road
33.1 Bear right on Southtown Road at Y intersection with Heller Road
34.1 Turn left at the end of Southtown Road onto CR 519 (unmarked)
35.5 Turn right onto Ackerson Road
36.9 Turn left onto CR 608/Silver Lake Road
37.2 Turn right onto Camp Wasigan Road
37.4 Turn left onto Golden Chain Road
38.2 Golden Chain Road becomes Mud Pond Road
39.5 Turn right onto CR 521/Hope Road
40.3 Turn left onto Union Brick Road
40.9 Turn right onto Heller Hill Road
41.6 Turn left onto Dry Road
43.0 Turn right onto Belcher Road
44.1 Turn right onto CR 616/Cedar Lake Road
44.3 Bear left onto Lambert Road
44.4 Turn left onto Airport Road and end tour at Blairstown Airport parking area

Option (from mile 21.4)
0.0 Turn left onto Goodale Road
2.9 Turn right onto Lake Iliff Road (unmarked)
3.8 Turn right onto CR 669/Limecrest Road
6.5 Turn left onto US 206 and continue from mile 21.4

0.2 Turn left at the end of Airport Road onto CR 616/Cedar Lake Road.

2.3 Turn left at the stop sign at the end of Cedar Lake Road onto CR 521/NJ 94.

2.5 Turn right at the traffic light onto CR 521 north/Stillwater Road.

4.7 Turn right onto CR 659 east/Spring Valley Road.
There's a short, steep climb here just before NJ 94.

6.0 Turn left onto NJ 94 north at the stop sign.

6.3 Take the first left onto Lincoln Laurel Road.
This road follows a ridge that offers pleasant views of the Delaware Water Gap Recreational Area just to the west. Along the route here the ride crosses over from Warren County into Sussex County.

8.2 Go straight onto Fredon Road (which becomes Marksboro Road).
Just past this intersection is Water Mill Farm. This picturesque setting is definitely a wonderful photo opportunity.

11.4 Turn right onto Warner Road.

12.4 Turn right onto NJ 94 at the stop sign.

12.9 Take the first left onto Fredon-Greendell Road.

14.2 At the stop sign go straight across CR 519 onto CR 608 east/Shotwell Road.
Here, the ride passes alongside the Whitingham Wildlife Management Area, where there are many trails leading into the woodlands.

16.1 Turn left onto CR 611/Wolfs Corner Road (which becomes Springdale-Greendell Road).

19.1 Turn right onto US 206 south.
There's traffic on US 206 into Andover, but the road has an adequate shoulder.

20.3 The Option turns left here onto Goodale Road.

21.4 Arrive in Andover and continue on US 206.
The Andover Diner is on the right. Before leaving town, US 206 passes through Andover Village Center, where there are quite a few opportunities to browse in antiques shops.

Cycling past late-summer corn

Leave Andover on US 206 south.

21.9 Turn right onto CR 517 south/Brighton Road/Tranquility Road (which becomes Decker Pond Road).

23.1 Turn left to continue on CR 517 south.

26.2 Turn right onto CR 611 north.

26.6 Turn left onto CR 668/Maple Lane/Cemetery Road.
The ride crosses back into Warren County here. The terrain becomes quite gentle, with wide uninterrupted views of the surrounding farmland.

28.0 Turn left at the end of CR 668/Maple Lane/Cemetery Road onto NJ 612 south/Johnsonburg Road.

28.5 Take the first right onto CR 615/Long Bridge Road.

29.4 Go straight to continue on Long Bridge Road at the intersection with Quaker Church Road.

29.7 Take the first right onto Shades of Death Road.

30.8 Bear right to continue on unmarked Shades of Death Road.

32.3 Before the highway overpass, turn right onto Southtown Road.
The riding here is surrounded by woodlands and becomes hillier.

33.1 Bear right on Southtown Road at the Y intersection with Heller Road.

34.1 Turn left at the stop sign at the end of Southtown Road onto unmarked CR 519 south.

35.5 Turn right onto Ackerson Road.
There's a general store 0.4 mile farther south on CR 519.

36.9 Turn left at the end of Ackerson Road onto CR 608/Silver Lake Road.

37.2 Turn right onto Camp Wasigan Road.

37.4 Turn left onto Golden Chain Road.

38.2 Golden Chain Road becomes Mud Pond Road.

39.5 Turn right at the end of Mud Pond Road onto CR 521/Hope Road.

40.3 Turn left onto Union Brick Road.

40.9 Turn right onto Heller Hill Road.

41.6 Turn left onto Dry Road.
Enjoy the views from this road toward the mountains of Pennsylvania in the west.

43.0 Turn right at the end of Dry Road onto Belcher Road.
Be careful on the winding downhill.

44.1 Turn right at the end of Belcher Road onto CR 616/Cedar Lake Road.

44.3 Bear left onto Lambert Road.

44.4 Turn left onto Airport Road and end the tour at the Blairstown Airport parking area.

Option

0.0 From mile 21.4 turn left onto Goodale Road.

2.9 Turn right onto unmarked Lake Iliff Road at the stop sign.

3.8 Turn right onto CR 669 south/Limecrest Road.
The ride passes the Kittatinny State Park and Airport, where there's a great deal of taking off and landing activity on weekends.

6.5 Turn left at the end of Limecrest Road onto US 206 south.
Continue from mile 21.4.

15

Somerset County

- **TOUR DISTANCE:** 37 miles
- **TERRAIN:** Moderate, with rolling terrain throughout and a few steeper climbs
- **SPECIAL FEATURES:** Leonard J. Buck Gardens, Oldwick Village, Pottersville Historic District, Gladstone

Although named Somerset County, this tour actually crosses into Tewksbury Township, which is located in Hunterdon County. Northern Somerset County is horse farm country, while the villages in Tewksbury have deep roots in early American history, with many of them listed on the National Register of Historic Places.

Pedaling starts from the local train station at Far Hills. We can get an immediate preview of the beauty of the countryside from the country estates that line the roads, each surrounded by meadows that sweep up into the nearby hills. At our first turn the ride passes the Leonard J. Buck Garden, a 33-acre naturalistic garden that features planted rock outcroppings with woodland trails rimmed with wildflowers. Leonard Buck, a trustee of the New York Botanical Gardens, bought the land in the 1930s and sculpted the garden from a glacial valley stream using chisels, shovels, and blasting to produce a woodland environment composed of many individual gardens, each with its own character. The gardens are at peak bloom in the spring.

The tour, tracing the gentle shoreline of the Lamington River, leads through the village of Pottersville, with its history dating from the mid-1700s. Many of the properties front the Black River and are typified by their Italianate and Queen Anne architecture. At this point the route crosses into one of the most rural sections of Hunterdon County. The landscape is dotted with small sheep and horse farms, many with old country barns. The village of Oldwick was originally named Smithfield by English settlers in 1734, and then was renamed New Germantown until it eventually came to be known by its current name. The first commercial structure in Oldwick was a general store, followed by a hotel and a tavern built by John Farley on land that he purchased from the Zion Lutheran Church. The church in the village was built by German American Lutherans in 1767 and remains prominent there today. A good choice for lunch is the Oldwick General Store, where there are picnic tables and bicycle racks in the rear as well as the opportunity to sit down inside.

Leaving Oldwick the route loops back through Pottersville and then climbs steadily through farmland on either side of the road. The headquarters of the U.S. Equestrian Team is located on Pottersville Road on the right, just before US 206. The U.S. Equestrian Center encourages individual and group visits to its training center. The stables were constructed in 1916 and have been described as some of largest and most lavish in the United States. The interior includes carriage and harness rooms with tile walls, terrazzo floors, and brass fittings. The trophy room, lined with walnut cases and stained-glass ceiling lights, displays the many ribbons and awards achieved by the team at the Olympics and in international competition.

Much of the cycling from here is in a gorgelike setting, following streams and lakes and leading back to Far Hills.

DRIVING DIRECTIONS   Take the New Jersey Turnpike to exit 14, I-78. Follow I-78 west for approximately 27 miles to I-287 north toward Morristown. Take I-287 to exit 22B, which leads to US 202/ US 206 north toward Bedminster. After about 1 mile on US 202 north, bear right toward Far Hills and Morristown. Turn right at the traffic light on US 202 north in Far Hills, and after about 0.75

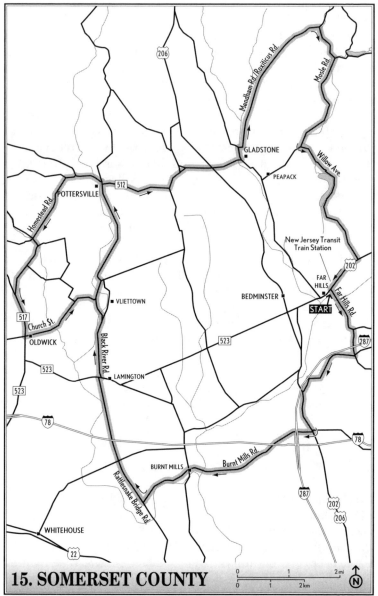

15. SOMERSET COUNTY

```
0        1          2 mi
0    1        2 km
```

Ⓝ

© The Countryman Press

0.0	Go straight from Far Hills Railroad Station parking area across US 202 onto Liberty Corners Road (becomes Far Hills Road)
1.0	Turn right onto Layton Road
1.5	Turn right onto Douglas Road
1.8	Bear right downhill onto Schley Mountain Road
2.8	Turn left onto access road to I-287, following the sign for US 202/US 206
3.2	Turn left onto US 202/US 206
3.9	Turn right onto Burnt Mills Road
7.9	Turn right onto CR 665/Rattlesnake Bridge Road
10.6	Turn right onto CR 523
	Turn left immediately onto Black River Road
12.1	Go straight to continue on Black River Road
14.4	Bear left onto CR 512/Pottersville Road
14.5	Bear left onto CR 512/Fairmount Road
14.7	Bear left to continue on CR 512/Fairmount Road
15.1	Turn left onto Hollow Brook Road
15.4	Turn left onto Homestead Road
16.8	Turn left at Cold Spring Road to continue on Homestead Road (unmarked)
18.2	Turn left onto CR 517/Old Turnpike Road (unmarked)
19.4	Arrive at four-way intersection in Oldwick
	Turn left onto Church Street (becomes Vliettown Road)
21.4	Turn left onto Black River Road at Y intersection with Vliettown Road
23.8	Turn right onto CR 512/Pottersville Road
26.2	Go straight across US 206 to continue on CR 512/Pottersville Road
26.7	Turn left onto Main Street in Gladstone
27.0	Turn right onto Jackson Avenue
	Turn left immediately onto Church Street
27.4	Merge left onto Mendham Road/Roxiticus Road
30.1	Turn right onto Union School House Road
30.8	Bear right onto Mosle Road at Y intersection with Union School House Road
31.5	Turn left onto Hub Hollow Road
33.0	Turn left onto Willow Avenue
33.6	Turn right onto Lake Road
34.8	Bear right where the road divides into one lane going each way
36.1	Turn right onto US 202
37.0	Turn right into Far Hills Railroad Station parking area

Early fall in rural New Jersey

mile turn left into the entrance of the Far Hills Railroad Station. The Far Hills train station can be reached by New Jersey Transit trains departing from Penn Station in New York City and from Hoboken, New Jersey.

The café at the Far Hills Railroad Station is open on Saturday morning and offers coffee and bathroom facilities. If you are taking this tour on a Saturday, don't park in the area in front of the station; it's reserved for customers of the restaurant.

Drive time from New York City is 55 minutes.

RIDE DIRECTIONS

0.0 Leaving the Far Hills Railroad Station, go straight across US 202 onto Liberty Corners Road (which becomes Far Hills Road).

1.0 Take the first right onto Layton Road.
The entrance to the Leonard Buck Garden is just after this turn on the left.

1.5 Turn right onto Douglas Road at the stop sign.

1.8 Bear right downhill at the yield sign onto Schley Mountain Road.

2.8 Turn left at the end of Schley Mountain Road onto the access road to I-287, following the sign for US 202/US 206.

3.2 Turn left onto US 202/US 206 at the traffic light.
Take care; there's traffic here for about 0.5 mile.

3.9 Turn right onto Burnt Mills Road at the traffic light.
The riding becomes much easier here as it follows the Lamington River.

7.9 Turn right at the end of Burnt Mills Road onto CR 665 north/Rattlesnake Bridge Road.
Again, there's easier riding here past some attractive horse farms.

10.6 Turn right onto CR 523 east.

Turn left immediately onto Black River Road.
This road parallels the Lamington River and leads to the historic hamlet of Pottersville.

12.1 Go straight to continue on Black River Road, passing Vlietown Road on the left.

14.4 Bear left at the yield sign onto CR 512/Pottersville Road.

14.5 Bear left downhill over the metal-grated bridge onto CR 512/Fairmount Road.
The Pottersville General Store is on the left just after the bridge. At this point the ride crosses into Hunterdon County and the terrain becomes hilly.

14.7 Bear left to continue on Fairmount Road.

15.1 Turn left onto Hollow Brook Road.
Watch for this turn; you'll be climbing a hill here. The rolling scenery here is pleasant, with small farms on either side of the route.

15.4 Turn left onto Homestead Road.

16.8 Turn left at Cold Spring Road to continue on unmarked Homestead Road.

18.2 Turn left onto unmarked CR 517/Old Turnpike Road.

19.4 Arrive at the main four-way intersection in Oldwick.
The Oldwick Store is on the right here. There's parking for bikes in the rear.

To leave Oldwick, turn left onto Church Street (which becomes Vliettown Road).

21.4 Turn left onto Black River Road at the Y intersection with Vliettown Road.
Here the route repeats a short section into the hamlet of Pottersville.

23.8 Turn right in Pottersville onto CR 512/Pottersville Road toward Gladstone.
The Peapack Gladstone Bank Building is on the left at this turn. From here the route climbs steadily. Just after the crest of the climb, the headquarters of the U.S. Equestrian Team is on the right.

26.2 Go straight across US 206 at the traffic light to continue on CR 512/Pottersville Road.

26.7 Turn left onto Main Street in Gladstone.

27.0 Turn right onto Jackson Avenue, following the sign for Mendham.

Turn left immediately onto Church Street.

27.4 Merge left at the stop sign onto Mendham Road/Roxiticus Road.

30.1 Turn right onto Union School House Road.
Be careful; this turn comes on a downhill and is easy to miss. Look for a white shed with a red roof here. The next 6 miles on this route provide some of the most scenic cycling to be found in all of New Jersey or anywhere else.

30.8 Bear right at the schoolhouse onto Mosle Road at the Y intersection with Union School House Road.

31.5 Turn left onto Hub Hollow Road at the bottom of the hill.
Because this turn is also on a downhill, it's easy to miss.

33.0 Turn left at the end of Hub Hollow Road onto Willow Avenue.

33.6 Turn right onto Lake Road just after crossing the bridge.

34.8 Bear right where the road divides into one lane going each way.

36.1 Turn right onto US 202 at the stop sign.

37.0 Turn right after the railroad tracks into the Far Hills Railroad Station parking area.

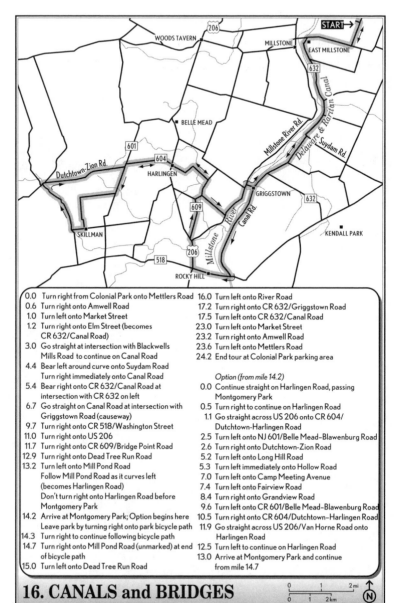

0.0	Turn right from Colonial Park onto Mettlers Road
0.6	Turn right onto Amwell Road
1.0	Turn left onto Market Street
1.2	Turn right onto Elm Street (becomes CR 632/Canal Road)
3.0	Go straight at intersection with Blackwells Mills Road to continue on Canal Road
4.4	Bear left around curve onto Suydam Road Turn right immediately onto Canal Road
5.4	Bear right onto CR 632/Canal Road at intersection with CR 632 on left
6.7	Go straight on Canal Road at intersection with Griggstown Road (causeway)
9.7	Turn right onto CR 518/Washington Street
11.0	Turn right onto US 206
11.7	Turn right onto CR 609/Bridge Point Road
12.9	Turn right onto Dead Tree Run Road
13.2	Turn left onto Mill Pond Road Follow Mill Pond Road as it curves left (becomes Harlingen Road) Don't turn right onto Harlingen Road before Montgomery Park
14.2	Arrive at Montgomery Park; Option begins here Leave park by turning right onto park bicycle path
14.3	Turn right to continue following bicycle path
14.7	Turn right onto Mill Pond Road (unmarked) at end of bicycle path
15.0	Turn left onto Dead Tree Run Road

16.0	Turn left onto River Road
17.2	Turn right onto CR 632/Griggstown Road
17.5	Turn left onto CR 632/Canal Road
23.0	Turn left onto Market Street
23.2	Turn right onto Amwell Road
23.6	Turn left onto Mettlers Road
24.2	End tour at Colonial Park parking area

Option (from mile 14.2)

0.0	Continue straight on Harlingen Road, passing Montgomery Park
0.5	Turn right to continue on Harlingen Road
1.1	Go straight across US 206 onto CR 604/Dutchtown-Harlingen Road
2.5	Turn left onto NJ 601/Belle Mead–Blawenburg Road
2.6	Turn right onto Dutchtown-Zion Road
5.2	Turn left onto Long Hill Road
5.3	Turn left immediately onto Hollow Road
7.0	Turn left onto Camp Meeting Avenue
7.4	Turn left onto Fairview Road
8.4	Turn right onto Grandview Road
9.6	Turn left onto CR 601/Belle Mead–Blawenburg Road
10.5	Turn right onto CR 604/Dutchtown–Harlingen Road
11.9	Go straight across US 206/Van Horne Road onto Harlingen Road
12.5	Turn left to continue on Harlingen Road
13.0	Arrive at Montgomery Park and continue from mile 14.7

16. CANALS and BRIDGES

Canals and Bridges

- **TOUR DISTANCE:** 24 miles (37 miles with Option)
- **TERRAIN:** Easy, with mostly flat terrain. The Option is moderate, with one very steep climb.
- **SPECIAL FEATURES:** Colonial Park Arboretum, Delaware and Raritan Canal State Park

This is an easy ride along the Delaware and Raritan Canal in southern Somerset County. One of America's oldest counties, Somerset was established in 1688 and is deeply rooted in Colonial and Revolutionary War history.

The ride begins in Colonial Park and Gardens, a 144-acre park with an arboretum and a perennial garden providing year-round interest for the enjoyment of gardeners and park visitors. A gazebo in the center of the garden is surrounded by beds that display a wide variety of flowering bulbs, perennials, and flowering trees and shrubs.

Just 1 mile into the route the cycling leads through the hamlet of East Millstone, where we can stop at a general store. A few more turns of the pedals lead cyclists to the Delaware and Raritan Canal. This 70-mile trail is one of central New Jersey's most popular recreational corridors for canoeing, jogging, hiking, and fishing. During the early 19th century, when America was entering the industrial revolution, canals were dug—often by hand—as transportation routes to link resources, manufacturing centers, and markets. For nearly a century the D and R Canal was one of

America's busiest navigation canals, transporting coal from Pennsylvania to New York on barges pulled by teams of mules or steam tugboats.

We can cycle here on the paved road that parallels the canal or cross the canal on any one of a number of bridges and cycle on the unpaved-yet-maintained towpath surface on the far side. The route passes the villages of Blackwells Mills and Griggstown, where we can discover reminders of this area's active past. There are a bridge tender's house, a mule tender's barracks and canal museum, and quite a few old wooden bridges crossing the canal along the route. Canoes can be rented on Canal Road just before the Griggstown crossing.

Just beyond Rocky Hill, lunch can be purchased at a deli. A picnic lunch in Montgomery Park, which has many open fields and trails and is just 3 miles farther along the route, is a good choice.

The Option on this tour leads out to and back from Montgomery Park and is a hilly ride with one steep climb. The route here is quiet and rural, continuing along sections of the Black Brook. Grandview Road is appropriately named; it provides a thrilling descent with spectacular views.

DRIVING DIRECTIONS   Take the New Jersey Turnpike to exit 14, I-78. Take I-78 west approximately 27 miles to I-287 south toward Somerville. Continue on I-287 south approximately 9 miles to exit 12, Weston Canal Road, Manville. Turn left at the stop sign onto Weston Canal Road and continue for 2.4 miles. Turn left onto Schoolhouse Road. Turn right onto Mettlers Road. Turn right and then make an immediate left to continue on Mettlers Road. Turn right into parking area F at the Colonial Park Arboretum.

There are bathrooms at the rear of the parking area.

Drive time from New York City is about one hour.

RIDE DIRECTIONS

0.0 Turn right from Colonial Park Arboretum onto Mettlers Road.

0.6 Turn right at the end of Mettlers Road onto Amwell Road.

We prefer to be surrounded by things that we love—bicycles!

1.0 Turn left onto Market Street after the blinking light.
There's a small market store here just before the D and R Canal.

1.2 Turn right at the stop sign at the end of Market Street onto Elm Street
(which becomes CR 632/Canal Road).
This road leads down to the canal.

3.0 Go straight at the intersection with Blackwells Mills Road to continue on
Canal Road.
*There are an old bridge tender's house, a wooden bridge, and a mill site here. The
canal trail can be accessed here by turning right and crossing the wooden bridge
and then turning left onto the canal trail.*

4.4 Bear left around the curve in the road here onto Suydam Road.

Turn right immediately onto Canal Road.

5.4 Bear right onto CR 632/Canal Road at the intersection with CR 632 on
the left.

6.7 Go straight on Canal Road at the intersection with Griggstown Road (causeway).

A mule tender's barracks and canal museum and a bridge tender's house are located here. Seasonal canoe rentals are available as well. There is also another wooden bridge crossing the canal, giving cyclists the option to cross over and cycle on the unpaved trail on the other side of the canal. One mile south of here the route passes the Griggstown Canal Lock.

9.7 Turn right at the traffic light onto CR 518 west/Washington Street.
Note that there's some traffic on this road.

11.0 Turn right onto US 206 toward Sommerville.
The WaWa Deli is on the corner at this turn. Sandwiches can be purchased here for a picnic lunch at Montgomery Park. Friendly's Restaurant, where you can have a full-service lunch, is located in the shopping center just beyond the WaWa Deli. Note that there's heavier traffic on US 206, but there's also a wide shoulder on the road.

11.7 Turn right onto CR 609/Bridge Point Road.

12.9 Turn right onto Dead Tree Run Road.

13.2 Turn left onto Mill Pond Road after the small bridge.
Follow Mill Pond as it curves left, becoming Harlingen Road; don't turn right onto Harlingen Road before Montgomery Park!

14.2 Arrive at Montgomery Park and turn left into the park's main entrance.
The park has picnic tables and miles of trails leading from the picnic area. The bathrooms are only opened when an event is held at the park, but there's a portable bathroom available at all times. The Option starts and finishes here.

Leave the park by turning right on the small bicycle path that begins on the other side of the car parking area opposite the picnic area.

14.3 Turn right to continue following the bicycle path.

14.7 Turn right onto unmarked Mill Pond Road at the end of the bicycle path.

15.0 Turn left at the end of Mill Pond Road onto Dead Tree Run Road.

16.0 Turn left at the end of Dead Tree Run Road onto River Road.
This road runs parallel to the canal on the canal's western bank.

17.2 Turn right onto CR 632/Griggstown Road.
There's a narrow bridge at this turn leading across the canal to the Griggstown site.

17.5 Turn left at the end of Griggstown Road onto CR 632/Canal Road.

23.0 Turn left onto Market Street, passing Chester's Market Store.

23.2 Turn right onto Amwell Road.

23.6 Turn left onto Mettlers Road toward Colonial Park Arboretum.

24.2 Turn left into parking area F at Colonial Park Arboretum to end the tour.

Option

0.0 From mile 14.2 continue straight on Harlingen Road, passing the main entrance to Montgomery Park.
If you've turned into the park for lunch, turn left when you leave the park to begin the Option.

0.5 Turn right to continue on Harlingen Road.

1.1 Go straight across US 206 onto CR 604/Dutchtown-Harlingen Road.

2.5 Turn left at the end of Dutchtown-Harlingen Road onto CR 601/Belle Mead–Blawenburg Road.

2.6 Take the first right onto Dutchtown-Zion Road.
There are both a steep uphill here and a short section of unpaved road just before the left turn.

5.2 Turn left at the stop sign at the end of Dutchtown-Zion Road onto Long Hill Road.

5.3 Turn left immediately onto Hollow Road.
Hollow Road is well paved, downhill, and runs along the Black Brook. It's a wonderful road to cycle on.

7.0 Turn left onto Camp Meeting Avenue.

7.4 Take the first left onto Fairview Road.

8.4 Turn right at the end of Fairview Road onto Grandview Road.
This is a great downhill run with breathtaking views.

9.6 Turn left at the stop sign at the end of Grandview Road onto CR 601/
Belle Mead–Blawenburg Road.

10.5 Turn right onto CR 604 east/Dutchtown-Harlingen Road.

11.9 Go straight across US 206/Van Horne Road onto Harlingen Road.

12.5 Turn left to continue on Harlingen Road.

13.0 Arrive in Montgomery.
Continue from mile 14.7.

17

Deer Path to Oldwick

- **TOUR DISTANCE:** 39 miles (48 miles with Option)
- **TERRAIN:** Moderate to more difficult, with rolling terrain throughout and a few longer, steeper grades in the second half of the ride
- **SPECIAL FEATURES:** Oldwick Village, Mountainville Village, Round Valley Reservoir

This loop departs from Deer Path Park and follows scenic country roads that lace their way through central Hunterdon County. Throughout the ride cyclists pass working farms, flowing streams, a picturesque river gorge, and villages that are listed on the National Register of Historic Places.

Rolling countryside leads to the Stanton General Store, where the muffins are among the largest and best ever made.

Oldwick center is located at the junctions of CR 523/CR 517 and Church and King Streets. The church standing at this intersection across from the General Store was built by German American Lutherans in 1767 and remains prominent in the village today. From the General Store there's an 8.6-mile hilly ride that loops out and back to Oldwick, passing through one of the most rural sections of Hunterdon County. The landscape here is sprinkled with small sheep and horse farms.

Leaving Oldwick, the route climbs briefly and then descends into the Rockaway River Gorge. The flowing river leads the way as the tour meanders across two small steel-deck bridges on either

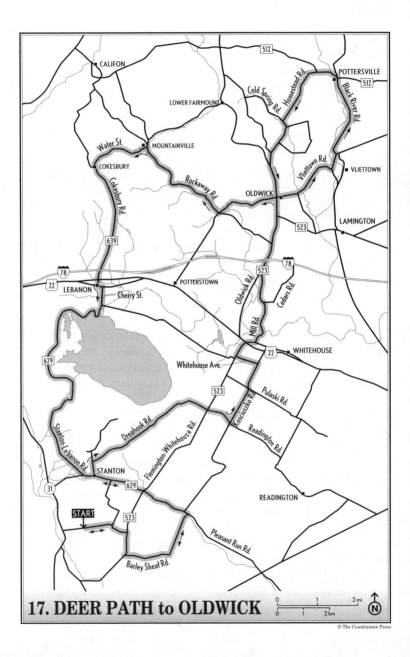

17. DEER PATH to OLDWICK

CALIFON
512
POTTERSVILLE
512
Homestead Rd.
Cold Spring Rd.
LOWER FAIRMOUNT
Black River Rd.
Water St.
MOUNTAINVILLE
Vliettown Rd.
VLIETTOWN
COKESBURY
Rockaway Rd.
OLDWICK
Cokesbury Rd.
LAMINGTON
639
523
78
78
22
LEBANON
POTTERSTOWN
523
Cherry St.
Oldwick Rd.
Cedars Rd.
629
Mill Rd.
Whitehouse Ave.
22
WHITEHOUSE
523
Kosciuszko Rd.
Pulaski Rd.
Stanton-Lebanon Rd.
Dreahook Rd.
Readington Rd.
Flemington-Whitehouse Rd.
STANTON
629
READINGTON
31
523
START
Pleasant Run Rd.
Barley Sheaf Rd.

0   1   2 mi
0   1   2 km

N

© The Countryman Press

0.0	Leave Deer Path Park parking area toward park exit
0.4	Turn right onto West Woodschurch Road
1.2	Turn right onto Woodschurch Road
1.6	Turn right onto CR 523/Flemington-Whitehouse Road (unmarked)
2.2	Turn left onto Barley Sheaf Road
4.5	Turn left onto CR 629/Pleasant Run Road
5.8	Go straight across CR 523 onto CR 629/Stanton Road
7.1	Turn right onto Stanton Mountain Road
7.5	Turn right onto Dreahook Road
10.9	Go straight onto East Dreahook Road
11.1	Turn right onto CR 620/Readington Road
11.8	Turn left onto Kosciuszko Road
12.8	Go straight across Pulaski Road onto School Road
13.4	Turn left onto Whitehouse Avenue
14.0	Turn right onto CR 523/Main Street
14.4	Go straight across US 22 onto CR 624
14.7	Turn left onto Mill Road
15.8	Bear left onto New Bromley Road at Y intersection with Cedars Road
16.6	Turn right onto CR 523/Oldwick Road (becomes CR 517/Oldwick Road)
18.5	Arrive in Oldwick at intersection of Church Street and King Street
	Turn left onto King Street; Option begins here
20.2	Turn right onto Rockaway Road
23.0	Turn left in Mountainville onto Main Street (becomes Water Street)
24.6	Go straight onto Cokesbury Road (unmarked)
27.5	Go straight across US 22
27.7	Arrive in Lebanon and turn left onto Main Street
27.9	Turn right onto Cherry Street
29.7	Turn left onto CR 629/Stanton-Lebanon Road (unmarked)
35.0	Pass Stanton General Store (often closed in the afternoon)
36.4	Turn right onto CR 523/Flemington-Whitehouse Road
37.5	Turn right onto Woodschurch Road
37.9	Turn left onto West Woodschurch Road
38.7	Turn left into Deer Path Park
39.1	End tour at parking area

Option (from mile 18.5)

0.0	Turn right in Oldwick onto Church Street/Vliettown Road
2.0	Turn left onto Black River Road
4.4	Bear left onto CR 512/ Fairmount Road
4.9	Turn left onto Hollow Brook Road
5.2	Turn left onto Homestead Road
6.6	Turn left at Cold Spring Road to continue on Homestead Road (unmarked)
8.1	Turn left onto CR 517/Old Turnpike Road/Oldwick Road
8.6	Arrive at Church Street and King Street intersection in Oldwick and continue from mile 18.5

side of the river. As the cycling passes Hill and Dale Road, note the beautiful horse farm on the right. Leaving the gorge, the road climbs gradually as riverside homes of exceptional beauty mark the way to the historic district of Mountainville. Pedaling through this small village takes us immediately back more than two hundred years to when the village was established in the mid-1700s. The expansion of the village began in the mid-1800s, when Daniel Potter, prominent in the founding of Pottersville, moved the Bull's Head Tavern from his farm and attached it to a home here. Other developments followed shortly thereafter: The Mountainville Academy was founded in 1832; two general stores were opened in the village, one in 1850 by Hiram Lindaberry and the other in 1869; and a carriage factory and wheelwright's shop opened in 1870. The village eventually became a small summer resort area, where vacationers lived with local families or stayed at the Mountainville Hotel or Lindaberry's Boarding House. The hotel remained in business until the 1930s, and Farley's General Store, which opened

The sun dapples this quiet, rural New Jersey road.

in 1869, remained open until 1964. It has since been the home of a series of restaurants and eateries.

The afternoon ride continues with a climb up to the Round Valley Reservoir, a 55-billion-gallon water storage facility that was created by the construction of two dams and a dike, closing off gaps in a natural horseshoe-shaped valley. The seasonal activities here include swimming, fishing, scuba diving, and cycling and hiking on a challenging 18-mile single-track trail.

DRIVING DIRECTIONS   Take the New Jersey Turnpike to exit 14, I-78. Take I-78 west approximately 27 miles to I-287 south. Continue approximately 3 miles to the exit marked US 202/US 206 south. Continue onto US 202 south toward Flemington for about 9 miles and turn right toward the sign for Stanton onto unmarked Pleasant Run Road. Continue approximately 3.5 miles and turn left onto CR 523. After 1 mile turn right onto Woodschurch Road toward Deer Path Park. Turn left on West Woodschurch Road and continue about 1 mile, turning left into Deer Path Park. Continue to the rear parking area.

To return to New York City, retrace your steps to US 202. Turn onto US 202 south and continue to the first U-turn on the left, where you'll reverse direction, heading north on US 202. Follow the signs for I-287 north to I-78 east.

Bathrooms are located in the rear parking area of Deer Path Park.

Drive time from New York City is 1 hour and 15 minutes.

RIDE DIRECTIONS

0.0 Leave the Deer Path Park parking area and head toward the park exit.

0.4 Turn right onto West Woodschurch Road.

1.2 Turn right at the end of West Woodschurch Road onto Woodschurch Road.

1.6 Turn right at the end of Woodschurch Road onto unmarked CR 523/Flemington-Whitehouse Road.

2.2 Take the first left onto Barley Sheaf Road.

4.5 Turn left at the end of Barley Sheaf Road onto CR 629/Pleasant Run Road.

5.8 Go straight across CR 523 onto CR 629 west/Stanton Road.
The route here climbs to Stanton.

7.1 Turn right onto Stanton Mountain Road at the Stanton General Store.
Stop here to either purchase—or just look at—the muffins.

7.5 Take the first right onto Dreahook Road.
Enjoy the downhill run on this sun-dappled road.

10.9 Go straight at the traffic light onto East Dreahook Road.

11.1 Take the first right onto CR 620/Readington Road.

11.8 Turn left onto Kosciuszko Road.

12.8 Go straight across Pulaski Road onto School Road.

13.4 Turn left onto Whitehouse Avenue.

14.0 Turn right at the end of Whitehouse Avenue onto CR 523/Main Street.

14.4 Go straight across US 22 at the traffic light onto CR 624 north.

14.7 Turn left onto Mill Road (the signpost is on the left behind a tree).
There's an attractive black angus cattle farm at the small, metal-grated bridge.

15.8 Bear left onto New Bromley Road at the Y intersection with Cedars Road.

16.6 Turn right at the end of New Bromley Road onto CR 523/Oldwick Road (which becomes CR 517/Oldwick Road).

18.5 Arrive in Oldwick at the intersection of Church Street and King Street.
The Oldwick General Store is located here on the left. There are bike racks and outside seating at the rear. The Option turns right here onto Church Street.

To leave Oldwick, turn left onto King Street/Potterstown Road.

20.2 Turn right onto Rockaway Road at the stop sign.
The cycling route now follows the scenic Rockaway River Gorge. After passing Hill and Dale Road on the right, the route climbs to Mountainville.

23.0 In Mountainville turn left at the end of Rockaway Road onto Main Street (which becomes Water Street).
The route climbs out of this hamlet, leading to an exciting downhill run toward Lebanon.

24.6 Go straight onto unmarked Cokesbury Road toward Lebanon.

27.5 Go straight across US 22 at the traffic light.

27.7 Arrive in Lebanon and turn left onto Main Street.

27.9 Turn right onto Cherry Street.
There's a short, steep climb here leading to the Round Valley Reservoir.

29.7 Turn left at the end of Cherry Street onto unmarked CR 629/Stanton-Lebanon Road.

35.0 Continue on the Stanton-Lebanon Road, passing the Stanton General Store.
The store is most often closed in the afternoon.

36.4 Turn right at the stop sign onto CR 523 south/Flemington-Whitehouse Road.

37.5 Turn right onto Woodschurch Road toward Deer Path Park.

37.9 Turn left onto West Woodschurch Road.

38.7 Turn left into Deer Path Park.

39.1 Arrive at the parking area to end the tour.

Option

0.0 From mile 18.5 turn right in Oldwick onto Church Street/Vliettown Road.
There's a short, steep climb out of Oldwick, followed by a nice downhill run to Black River Road.

2.0 Turn left at the end of Church Street/Vliettown Road onto Black River Road.
This road leads through the historic hamlet of Pottersville.
4.4 Bear left uphill over the metal-grated bridge onto CR 512/Fairmount Road.
This route passes the Pottersville Deli.

4.9 Turn left onto Hollow Brook Road.
Watch carefully for this turn; you'll be cycling uphill and the signpost is on the left.

5.2 Take the first left onto Homestead Road.
The route is hilly here, but it's also extremely quiet and scenic as it returns you to Oldwick.

6.6 Turn left at Cold Spring Road to continue on unmarked Homestead Road.

8.1 Turn left onto CR 517/Old Turnpike Road/Oldwick Road.

8.6 Arrive at the Church Street and King Street intersection in Oldwick.
Continue from mile 18.5.

18

Frenchtown Treasures

- **TOUR DISTANCE:** 35 miles
- **TERRAIN:** Moderate, with rolling terrain and two short, steeper climbs
- **SPECIAL FEATURES:** Frenchtown, the Delaware and Raritan Bicycle Trail, Uhlerstown Covered Bridge

Although there has been some development in this area of Hunterdon County, the countryside along this tour still retains much of its natural beauty. It has been one of the flagship rides in our bicycling program. The ride starts from a nature preserve located beside the South Branch of the Raritan River. After a short warm-up ride along the river's western shore, the route climbs for about a mile, offering views across a picturesque valley. Rolling terrain with meadows and farms follows us into Frenchtown. This small village is a biker's haven, offering many different choices of cycling routes by virtue of its location beside the Delaware and Raritan Bicycle Trail and the Delaware River. Freeman's Bicycle Shop is located in the center of the village, along with a number of antiques shops and various cafés offering different lunch options. The Bridge Café is one worth recommending because of its location alongside the river and its wonderful homemade desserts.

After crossing the bridge to Pennsylvania, it's just 0.3 mile down Uhlerstown Road to the Uhlerstown Covered Bridge. It was built in 1832 in a town once called Mexico, though the town was renamed after Michael Uhler, who owned a line of canal boats and

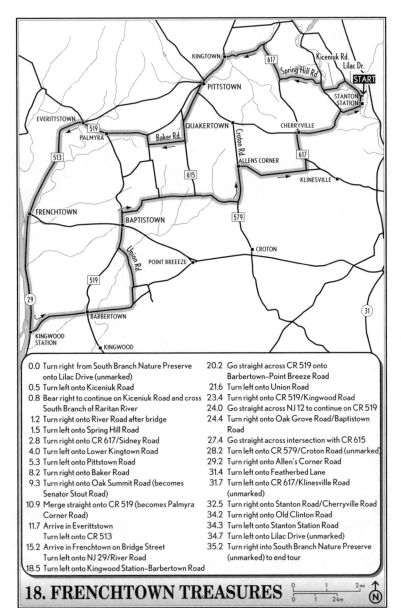

0.0 Turn right from South Branch Nature Preserve onto Lilac Drive (unmarked)	**20.2** Go straight across CR 519 onto Barbertown–Point Breeze Road
0.5 Turn left onto Kiceniuk Road	**21.6** Turn left onto Union Road
0.8 Bear right to continue on Kiceniuk Road and cross South Branch of Raritan River	**23.4** Turn right onto CR 519/Kingwood Road
1.2 Turn right onto River Road after bridge	**24.0** Go straight across NJ 12 to continue on CR 519
1.5 Turn left onto Spring Hill Road	**24.4** Turn right onto Oak Grove Road/Baptistown Road
2.8 Turn right onto CR 617/Sidney Road	**27.4** Go straight across intersection with CR 615
4.0 Turn left onto Lower Kingtown Road	**28.2** Turn left onto CR 579/Croton Road (unmarked)
5.3 Turn left onto Pittstown Road	**29.2** Turn right onto Allen's Corner Road
8.2 Turn right onto Baker Road	**31.4** Turn left onto Featherbed Lane
9.3 Turn right onto Oak Summit Road (becomes Senator Stout Road)	**31.7** Turn left onto CR 617/Klinesville Road (unmarked)
10.9 Merge straight onto CR 519 (becomes Palmyra Corner Road)	**32.5** Turn right onto Stanton Road/Cherryville Road
11.7 Arrive in Everittstown Turn left onto CR 513	**34.2** Turn right onto Old Clinton Road
	34.3 Turn left onto Stanton Station Road
15.2 Arrive in Frenchtown on Bridge Street Turn left onto NJ 29/River Road	**34.7** Turn left onto Lilac Drive (unmarked)
18.5 Turn left onto Kingwood Station–Barbertown Road	**35.2** Turn right into South Branch Nature Preserve (unmarked) to end tour

18. FRENCHTOWN TREASURES

had a country store at this location. With windows on both sides, it's the only bridge that crosses the Delaware Canal and the Canal Towpath. Cyclists completing this entire tour along with its optional short hops can feel quite satisfied that in only one day they've visited New Jersey, Pennsylvania, and Mexico.

Leaving Frenchtown, the ride continues on a flat route paralleling the Delaware for 3 miles before making a steady climb away from the river. The climb, the only uphill pedaling on the afternoon ride, is on a quiet country road beside a stream. For a short distance the road surface is unpaved. The remainder of the ride, about 15 miles, is on easy terrain with a steep downhill (be careful here!) just before completing the ride and returning to the parking area at the South Branch of the Raritan River.

DRIVING DIRECTIONS   Take the New Jersey Turnpike to exit 14, I-78. Take I-78 west to exit 17, Flemington, and follow the signs to NJ 31 south. Continue on NJ 31 south for about 4 miles and turn right onto Hibbler Road. Make a hard left onto Lilac Drive and continue 0.8 mile to the South Branch Nature Preserve. Turn left into the Echo Hill parking area at the preserve.

To return to New York City, leave the Echo Hill parking area and turn left onto Lilac Drive. Turn left onto Stanton Station Road and then left again at the traffic light onto NJ 31 north.

To reach the bathrooms in the preserve, walk across the meadow just behind the parking area toward the building down the hill.

Drive time from New York City is 1 hour and 10 minutes.

RIDE DIRECTIONS

0.0 Turn right from the South Branch Nature Preserve onto unmarked Lilac Drive.

0.5 Turn left onto Kiceniuk Road.
Carefully cross the railroad tracks.

0.8 Bear right to continue on Kiceniuk Road, cycling across the South Branch of the Raritan River.

1.2 Turn right at the end of Kiceniuk Road onto River Road after the bridge.

1.5 Take the first left uphill onto Spring Hill Road or continue straight on River Road to the first bridge and return to turn right onto Spring Hill Road. *This alternative is a 2.5-mile out-and-back—a very pretty and quiet ride along the river. Spring Hill Road climbs steadily, with some lovely valley views off to the right. There are two short, steeper grades on Spring Hill Road.*

2.8 Turn right at the end of Spring Hill Road onto CR 617/Sidney Road.

4.0 Turn left onto Lower Kingtown Road and continue right across the bridge. *Be careful turning onto Lower Kingtown Road; it's a blind turn on a downhill. For safety, walk this turn.*

5.3 Turn left at the stop sign at the end of Lower Kingtown Road onto Pittstown Road. *There is increased traffic on this road until it reaches Pittstown.*

6.3 The Pittstown Inn on the right has bathrooms.

8.2 Turn right onto Baker Road.

9.3 Turn right at the end of Baker Road onto Oak Summit Road (which becomes Senator Stout Road).

10.9 Merge straight onto CR 519 (which becomes Palmyra Corner Road).

11.7 Arrive in Everittstown and turn left onto CR 513 south at the stop sign. *There is a short, very steep downhill here into Frenchtown.*

15.2 Arrive in Frenchtown on Bridge Street. *Although there are a few lunch choices in the village, the best bet is the Bridge Café. To visit the Uhlerstown Covered Bridge, cross the bridge over the Delaware River and turn left at the end, then immediately turn right onto Uhlerstown Covered Bridge Road. The bridge is 0.3 mile down the road.*

Leave Frenchtown on NJ 29 south/River Road, alongside Freeman's Bicycle Shop.

18.5 Turn left onto Kingwood Station–Barbertown Road. *This is an easy turn to miss; the road is narrow and the signpost is on the left. This* *pretty road climbs away from the Delaware River and includes a short unpaved section.*

20.2 Go straight across CR 519 onto Barbertown–Point Breeze Road.

21.6 Turn left onto Union Road.

23.4 Turn right onto CR 519/Kingwood Road.

24.0 Go straight across NJ 12 at the traffic light to continue on CR 519.

24.4 Turn right onto Oak Grove Road/Baptistown Road.

27.4 Go straight across the intersection with CR 615.

28.2 Turn left onto unmarked CR 579/Croton Road.

29.2 Turn right onto Allen's Corner Road.

31.4 Turn left onto Featherbed Lane.

31.7 Turn left at the stop sign at the end of Featherbed Lane onto unmarked CR 617/Klinesville Road.

32.5 Turn right onto Stanton Road/Cherryville Road at the sign on the left pointing to Quakertown.
Take care; there's a very steep downhill run on this road just before the turn at mile 34.2.

34.2 Turn right onto Old Clinton Road at the stop sign at the end of Stanton Road/Cherryville Road.

34.3 Turn left onto Stanton Station Road.

34.7 Turn left onto unmarked Lilac Drive at Stanton Station Country Store and immediately after the railroad tracks.
You may be able to purchase a cold drink here from a cooler that's left in front of the store. Just leave your payment for the drink.

35.2 Turn right into the unmarked South Branch Nature Preserve to end the tour.

19

The Delaware's Banks

- **TOUR DISTANCE:** 26 miles (42 miles with Option)
- **TERRAIN:** Easy to moderate, with one steep climb at the beginning of the route. The Option is moderate, with rolling terrain throughout.
- **SPECIAL FEATURES:** Milford, New Jersey; Riegelsville, Pennsylvania

This is a quiet route that leads over shaded roads with dappled light and through stream-lined ravines bordered by groves of hemlock. Starting in the village of Bloomsbury, the ride quickly climbs a steep ridge after which there's a long, pleasant, gradual descent all the way to the Delaware River. The cycling leads through the hamlet of Little York in Holland Township, where there's a charming cluster of old stone homes. Because of its rural nature—dense woodlands, flowing streams, and hilly terrain— there are still many small farms operating here today.

The road soon leads to Milford, New Jersey, a quiet village nestled in the Delaware Valley, where it has managed to avoid the effects of urbanization and tourism. A short pause is in order here: In town there are interesting shops and a great bakery with wonderful pastries. Just before the bridge crossing the Delaware River there are a striking Victorian railroad station and an old gristmill, which at one time was the center of life here. As we leave Milford on Church Street, we can look to the left and see the River's Edge

Farm Market set back from the road. Here fresh seasonal fruits and vegetables can be purchased.

The cycling continues on a flat route along the eastern shore of the Delaware River. It's interesting to note that after a rainstorm, water cascades at intervals down the rocky face of the cliffs that follow the roadside, creating a cooling change in temperature.

Just before arriving in Riegelsville the cycling route turns left onto Old River Road, passing the Parsley's Ferry Historic District. This small ferry operated from a tavern located here in the mid-1700s and crossed the Delaware from the mouth of the Musconet-cong River in New Jersey to Durham, Pennsylvania. The ferry ceased operations when the Roebling-designed bridge spanning the Delaware at Riegelsville was constructed in 1837. On the weekends a sit-down lunch is a good choice at the Riegelsville Hotel and Inn, located beside the river in Pennsylvania. Lunch service is usually quick and there's a free pastry buffet set up in an adjoining dinning room.

Returning to New Jersey, the ride crosses from Hunterdon to Warren County for a shorter return back to Bloomsbury. The Option on the tour is hillier, providing many exceptional views of the rural countryside.

DRIVING DIRECTIONS   Take the New Jersey Turnpike south to exit 14, I-78. Take I-78 west to exit 7. Bear right onto NJ 173 west, continuing under the interstate underpass. Stop at the auto-truck stop for bathrooms. Bear left immediately after the auto-truck stop onto Main Street toward Bloomsbury. (There's a little park on the corner here.) Continue 0.2 mile to the parking area opposite the Bloomsbury Rescue Squad.

Drive time from New York City is 1 hour and 15 minutes.

RIDE DIRECTIONS

0.0 Leaving the parking area opposite the Bloomsbury Rescue Squad, turn left onto Main Street.

0.4 Turn right at the end of Main Street onto Church Street.

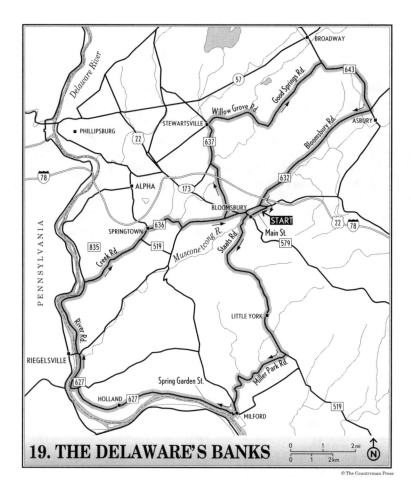

19. THE DELAWARE'S BANKS

0.0 Turn left onto Main Street from parking area opposite Bloomsbury Rescue Squad
0.4 Turn right onto Church Street
0.5 Turn left onto Willow Avenue
0.9 Bear left onto Milford Road
1.1 Turn right onto Staats Road (becomes Myler Road)
3.2 Turn right onto Sweet Hollow Road
4.6 Go straight onto CR 614
4.9 Bear left onto CR 631/Little York Road
6.0 Turn right onto Miller Park Road
7.9 Turn left onto Javes Road (becomes York Road)
8.9 Turn left onto Mill Street in Milford
9.1 Turn left onto Water Street
9.2 Turn right onto Bridge Street
9.3 Turn right onto Church Street
9.4 Turn right onto CR 627/Spring Garden Street (becomes Riegelsville-Milford Road)
14.6 Turn left onto River Road
16.3 Turn left onto CR 627
16.5 Turn left to arrive at bridge across Delaware River
16.7 Enter Riegelsville, Pennsylvania, after crossing bridge
     Reverse direction to return to New Jersey via bridge
17.0 On New Jersey side of bridge, turn left onto River Road
19.7 Turn right onto Creek Road
20.9 Turn left to continue on Creek Road
22.1 Turn left onto CR 519 (unmarked)
22.5 Turn right onto CR 636/Municipal Drive
23.8 Turn left onto CR 639
25.3 Pass CR 637/Maple Drive on left; Option begins here
25.8 Turn right onto NJ 173
25.9 Turn right onto Church Street and cross bridge into Bloomsbury
26.0 Turn left onto Main Street at school
26.4 Turn right into parking area opposite Rescue Squad to end tour

     Option (from mile 25.3)
0.0 Turn left onto CR 637/Maple Drive
0.3 Go straight across NJ 173 to continue on CR 637
3.1 Turn right onto CR 638/Washington Sreet in Stewartsville
3.5 Turn right onto Willow Grove Road
3.9 Bear left at Y intersection with Herleman Road to continue on
     Willow Grove Road (unmarked)
5.5 Turn left onto Good Springs Road
8.0 Turn right onto CR 643/Asbury Road
10.5 Turn right onto CR 632/Bloomsbury Road
15.3 Turn left onto NJ 173
15.4 Turn right onto Wilson Street (unmarked) and cross Brunswick Avenue
15.5 Turn right onto Main Street in Bloomsbury
15.6 Turn left into parking area opposite Rescue Squad

0.5 Turn left onto Willow Avenue, continuing under the railroad overpass.

0.9 Bear left uphill onto Milford Road.
A steep 1-mile-plus uphill climb begins here and continues to where Staats Road becomes Myler Road.

1.1 Turn right at the end of Milford Road onto Staats Road (which becomes Myler Road).
Myler Road marks the beginning of a long, gentle downhill. The road is sun-dappled and lined with flowing streams.

3.2 Turn right at the end of Myler Road onto Sweet Hollow Road.

4.6 Go straight onto CR 614 west.

4.9 Bear left onto CR 631 south/Little York Road.

6.0 Turn right onto Miller Park Road.
This is another sun-dappled, stream-lined road, but this one becomes unpaved until it reaches Javes Road.

The River's Edge Farm Market in Milford displays colorful produce.

7.9 Turn left at the end of Miller Park Road onto Javes Road (which becomes York Road).

8.9 Turn left onto Mill Street in Milford before the busy highway.

9.1 Turn left at the end of Mill Street onto Water Street.

9.2 Turn right onto Bridge Street at the traffic light.
The route enters the village of Milford here. The bakery on the left after the turn makes good coffee and wonderful pastries and muffins.

9.3 Turn right onto Church Street at the bank and then left at the church.
There's often a fresh farmer's market on the left, set back from the road, just before the left turn at the church.

9.4 Turn right onto CR 627/Spring Garden Street (which becomes Riegelsville-Milford Road).
This pleasant, flat road follows the bank of the Delaware River. It's also bordered by a shale cliff face that rises up from the road. After a rainfall water will often cascade down the sheer face of the shale rocks, creating interesting effects.

14.6 Turn left onto Old River Road, opposite Church Road.
This lane leads back to the Delaware River through the Parsley's Ferry Historic District.

16.3 Turn left at the end of Old River Road onto CR 627 north.

16.5 Turn left at the stop sign to arrive at the bridge spanning the Delaware River.
Be careful crossing the bumpy railroad tracks.

16.7 Arrive at the bridge spanning the Delaware River.
The bridge is an attractive 19th-century Roebling bridge. Walk your bike on the walkway of the bridge, crossing the Delaware to Riegelsville, Pennsylvania. The Riegelsville Hotel and Inn is just beside the bridge. Lunch!

Leave Riegelsville by crossing the bridge back into New Jersey.

17.0 On the New Jersey side of the river, turn left onto River Road toward Carpentersville.
The route follows the bank of the Delaware River.

19.7 Turn right onto Creek Road after the green bridge.
The unmarked road here is bordered by small farms and streams that flow toward the Delaware River.

20.9 Turn left at the intersection with Mountain Road on the right to continue on Creek Road.

22.1 Turn left at the end of Creek Road onto unmarked CR 519.

22.5 Turn right onto CR 636 east/Municipal Drive.

23.8 Turn left at the end of Municipal Drive onto CR 639 east.

25.3 Pass CR 637/Maple Drive on the left.
The Option turns left onto Maple Drive.

25.8 Turn right onto NJ 173 east.

25.9 Turn right onto Church Street and cross the bridge into Bloomsbury.

26.0 Turn left at the school onto Main Street.

26.4 Turn right into the parking area opposite the Rescue Squad to end the tour.

Option

0.0 From mile 25.3 turn left onto CR 637/Maple Drive.

0.3 Go straight across NJ 173 to continue on CR 637.
The ride is generally quite easy here as it heads toward Stewartsville. As the road winds gently downhill, you'll see some old stone buildings and farms beside the route.

3.1 Turn right onto CR 638/Washingreet in Stewartsville.
From this point on the terrain is rolling, with only one steeper climb. The route is a quiet ride, offering broad views of northwestern New Jersey's farm country.

3.5 Turn right onto Willow Grove Road.

3.9 Bear left at the Y intersection with Herleman Road to continue on unmarked Willow Grove Road.

5.5 Turn left onto Good Springs Road.
The cycling on this road is quite picturesque, with the landscape rolling to a valley-like setting framed by a ridge of hills.

8.0 Turn right at the end of Good Springs Road onto CR 643 south/Asbury Road.
The more difficult climb begins here.

10.5 Turn right onto CR 632 west/Bloomsbury Road.
Asbury Willow General Store on the left just before the turn is a good rest stop. They serve good coffee and pastries and also have a bathroom available.

15.3 Turn left at the end of Bloomsbury Road onto NJ 173 east.

15.4 Turn right onto unmarked Wilson Street and cross Brunswick Avenue.

15.5 Turn right onto Main Street in Bloomsbury.

15.6 Turn left into the parking lot opposite the Bloomsbury Rescue Squad.

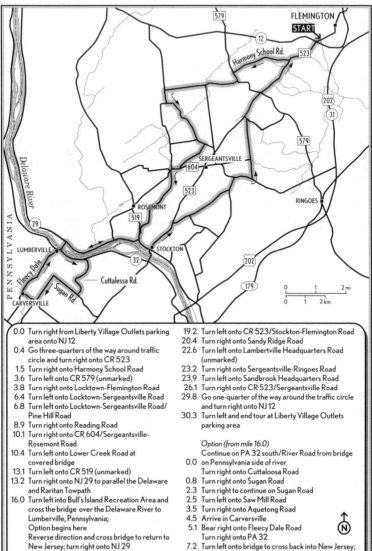

0.0 Turn right from Liberty Village Outlets parking area onto NJ 12	19.2 Turn left onto CR 523/Stockton-Flemington Road
0.4 Go three-quarters of the way around traffic circle and turn right onto CR 523	20.4 Turn right onto Sandy Ridge Road
1.5 Turn right onto Harmony School Road	22.6 Turn left onto Lambertville Headquarters Road (unmarked)
3.6 Turn left onto CR 579 (unmarked)	23.2 Turn right onto Sergeantsville-Ringoes Road
3.8 Turn right onto Locktown-Flemington Road	23.9 Turn left onto Sandbrook Headquarters Road
6.4 Turn left onto Locktown-Sergeantsville Road	26.1 Turn right onto CR 523/Sergeantsville Road
6.8 Turn left onto Locktown-Sergeantsville Road/ Pine Hill Road	29.8 Go one-quarter of the way around the traffic circle and turn right onto NJ 12
8.9 Turn right onto Reading Road	30.3 Turn left and end tour at Liberty Village Outlets parking area
10.1 Turn right onto CR 604/Sergeantsville-Rosemont Road	
10.4 Turn left onto Lower Creek Road at covered bridge	*Option (from mile 16.0)*
13.1 Turn left onto CR 519 (unmarked)	Continue on PA 32 south/River Road from bridge
13.2 Turn right onto NJ 29 to parallel the Delaware and Raritan Towpath	0.0 on Pennsylvania side of river
	Turn right onto Cuttalossa Road
16.0 Turn left into Bull's Island Recreation Area and cross the bridge over the Delaware River to Lumberville, Pennsylvania;	0.8 Turn right onto Sugan Road
	2.3 Turn right to continue on Sugan Road
Option begins here	2.5 Turn left onto Saw Mill Road
Reverse direction and cross bridge to return to New Jersey; turn right onto NJ 29	3.5 Turn right onto Aquetong Road
	4.5 Arrive in Carversville
18.5 Follow NJ 29 as it curves right	5.1 Bear right onto Fleecy Dale Road
	Turn right onto PA 32
	7.2 Turn left onto bridge to cross back into New Jersey;
	7.5 continue from mile 16.0

20. FLEMINGTON, NJ to LUMBERVILLE, PA

Flemington to Lumberville, Pennsylvania

- **TOUR DISTANCE:** 30 miles (38 miles with Option)
- **TERRAIN:** Easy to moderate, with longer flat sections, some rolling terrain, and two short but steeper climbs
- **SPECIAL FEATURES:** Flemington; Sergeantsville Covered Bridge; Prallsville Mill Site; Delaware River; historic Bucks County, Pennsylvania

This tour follows the country lanes of Hunterdon County, New Jersey, and Bucks County, Pennsylvania. Hunterdon County, located in western New Jersey, offers a network of back roads, bike trails, and charming villages that make it delightful for a day or more of cycle touring. The ride starts at the Liberty Village parking area in Flemington, New Jersey. Save some time for a stroll down Flemington's main street. You'll note the fascinating mix of Greek Revival and Victorian buildings here, where 60 percent of the buildings are on the National Register of Historical Places. The Hunterdon County Courthouse, a Greek Revival building, was the site of what some called the Trial of the Century, in which Bruno Hauptman was convicted for the kidnapping of the infant son of Charles Lindburgh.

This route continues past the last covered bridge in New Jersey, built in 1866. A little farther on, the Prallsville Mills complex, located beside the Delaware River and comprising a gristmill and eight other buildings, illustrates a village industrial scene typical of the late 1700s. The mill site is also the headquarters of the linear

Delaware and Raritan State Park Recreational Trail. This trail continues for 64 miles from Frenchtown to New Brunswick, New Jersey, and is used for cycling, walking, and jogging.

We continue on to Bull's Island Recreation Area, a 24-acre forested island with 69 tent and trailer campsites. The area is quite popular and is often fully booked on weekends during the summer season. At Bull's Island, we cross the Delaware River on a handsome footbridge to Lumberville, Pennsylvania, in historic Bucks County. The heart of the village is comprised of two rows of wonderfully maintained stone and frame homes, a church, a country store, and two inns. The Black Bass Inn, which stands alongside the bridge crossing the Delaware River, opened in 1740. It was run as a European-style country hotel and served as a country retreat for President Cleveland, who came to fish and find solitude here.

The Option on this tour follows a 7.5-mile loop into Bucks County. Cyclists pass Cutalooosa Farm in its unique setting that's reminiscent of a typical farm found in the English countryside. The ride continues through the hamlet of Carversville, and then onto Fleecy Dale Road. Here cyclists can glide gently downhill along Paunacussing Creek, passing lovely stone homes, before returning to the banks of the Delaware River. Carversville is listed on the National Register of Historic Places and in 1730 was a bustling village with five mills. Before the tour crosses the Delaware River back to New Jersey, we can note another recreational trail that borders the Delaware River in Pennsylvania. The canal located just beside the trail was dug by immigrants in the mid-1800s to be used as a mule and barge towpath. It begins at the confluence of the Lehigh and Delaware Rivers in Easton, Pennsylvania, and continues for 60 miles, passing Washington Crossing State Park. The history of the towpath, the canal, and its construction are displayed in a museum located in Easton, Pennsylvania.

DRIVING DIRECTIONS   Take the New Jersey Turnpike to exit 14, I-78. Take I-78 west for approximately 27 miles to I-287 south. Take I-287 south approximately 3 miles to US 202/US 206, which is a left exit. Continue on US 202 south toward Flemington. At the Flemington traffic circle continue one-quarter of the way around onto NJ 12 west. At the next traffic circle continue half of the way around, remaining on NY 12 west. Continue across the railroad tracks, passing Stengel Road on the right, which is the first entrance into the Liberty Village Outlet Shops at Flemington. Make the next right turn into the parking area and park next to the Park and Ride area alongside NJ 12.

There are public bathrooms located in the Liberty Village Outlet Shops at the end of the adjacent parking area.

Drive time from New York City is 1 hour and 15 minutes.

RIDE DIRECTIONS

0.0 Leaving the parking area exit ramp at the rear of the Liberty Village Outlet Shops parking area, turn right onto NJ 12 west.
There's some traffic on NJ 12, but the shoulder is wide enough here for safe cycling.

0.4 Go three-quarters of the way around the traffic circle onto CR 523 toward Stockton.
Again, there's some traffic here until the route gets away from Flemington.

1.5 Turn right onto Harmony School Road.
The signpost for this road is on the right, but you have to be looking for it. Harmony School Road has a short uphill just at the right turn and then becomes quite rural and quiet.

3.6 Turn left at the end of Harmony School Road onto unmarked CR 579.

3.8 Take the first right onto Locktown-Flemington Road.
This turn comes quickly, especially because you're cycling on a downhill. Locktown-Flemington Road is quite gentle, scenic, and sun-dappled.

6.4 Turn left at the end of Locktown-Flemington Road onto Locktown-Sergeantsville Road.

6.8 Take the first left onto Locktown-Sergeantsville Road/Pine Hill Road.
This road has a downhill run followed by a steady climb and a steep downhill with magnificent views of the countryside.

8.9 Turn right onto Reading Road.
You'll be coasting here and can easily miss this turn if you're not paying attention.

10.1 Turn right onto CR 604/Sergeantsville-Rosemont Road.
You'll arrive at the Sergeantsville covered bridge, which is New Jersey's last covered bridge.

10.4 Turn left onto Lower Creek Road just before the covered bridge.
The traffic goes through the bridge in only one direction and it's a blind turn, which means you must be alert. It's best to dismount here and walk. Enjoy Lower Creek Road; it's one of the most scenic roads in all New Jersey.

13.1 Turn left at the end of Lower Creek Road onto unmarked CR 519.

13.2 Turn right onto NJ 29, paralleling the Delaware and Raritan towpath.
There's a wide shoulder to enjoy riding on here. You'll be paralleling the D and R towpath and will likely see many cyclists pedaling along the path. If you were to turn left at NJ 29, you'd reach the historic Prallsville Mill Site on the right in 0.1 mile. If you were to continue another 0.7 mile in the same direction, you'd arrive in the village of Stockton. A nice restaurant called Miels is located at the main intersection there.

16.0 Turn left just past the Raven Rock sign and go across the white bridge into Bull's Island Recreation Area; continue to the bridge that crosses the Delaware River.
You'll have to walk across this bridge, which will take you onto PA 32 in Bucks County, Pennsylvania. Just to the left here is the historic Black Bass Inn—definitely worth a look. Its dining room overlooking the river is a possible lunch spot. Another is the Lumberville General Store, where they make excellent sandwiches and provide a nice picnic table outside, leaving you more time for cycling. The Option begins in Lumberville.

Cross the bridge back to New Jersey and turn right onto NJ 29 toward Stockton.
If you wish to cycle on the D and R towpath, turn right onto the gravel trail and follow it for about 3 miles to Main Street in Stockton. Turn left on Main Street and ride to the end, about 0.1 mile. Turn left onto NJ 29 north for about 0.1 mile. Turn right onto CR 523 toward Flemington. Continue the tour at mile 19.2.

18.5 Follow NJ 29 as it curves to the right.

19.2 Turn left onto CR 523/Stockton-Flemington Road.
This takes you uphill steeply at first, then steadily as you cycle away from the Delaware River.

20.4 Turn right onto Sandy Ridge Road.
You'll pass Sandy Ridge Church on this road that gives you pleasant views of the farmland and meadows that line the Delaware Valley.

22.6 Turn left at the end of Sandy Ridge Road onto unmarked Lambertville Headquarters Road.
There's a short, steep downhill at the end of the road.

23.2 Turn right at end of Lambertville Headquarters Road onto Sergeantsville-Ringoes Road.

23.9 Turn left onto Sandbrook Headquarters Road.
There's an impressive horse farm on the right at this turn. There have often been horse shows here at the turn onto Sandbrook Headquarters Road.

26.1 Turn right onto CR 523/Sergeantsville Road.
This road has rolling terrain with moderate traffic—you're now on the main road leading toward Flemington.

29.8 Turn right at the traffic circle and continue one-quarter of the way around the circle onto NJ 12 east.

30.3 Turn left into the parking area of the Liberty Village Outlet Shops to end the tour.
Because of the heavier traffic on this road, it's wise to walk your bike across NJ 12.

Option

0.0 From mile 16.0 leave the Lumberville General Store near the bridge on the Pennsylvania side of the river and continue on PA 32 south/River Road.

0.8 Turn right onto Cuttaloosa Road.
This road climbs as it leaves the Delaware River. Shortly you'll pass Cuttaloosa Farm, a complex of quaint buildings in an area on either side of the road that looks somewhat like the English countryside. There may be sheep or other animals on the grounds; you may offer them feed that's available for purchase. After Cuttaloosa Farm the road becomes gravel for about 0.7 mile.

2.3 Turn right onto Sugan Road.

2.5 Turn right to continue on Sugan Road.

3.5 Turn left onto Saw Mill Road at the NO OUTLET sign.

4.5 Turn right at the end of Saw Mill Road onto Aquetong Road.
This road leads to the scenic hamlet of Carversville, with its many stone buildings that are so typical in this area of Bucks County. There's a general store in Carversville on the right just before Fleecy Dale Road.

5.1 Arrive in Carversville and bear right onto Fleecy Dale Road.
Enjoy this gentle downhill pedal along one of the most scenic roads in Bucks County.

7.2 Turn right at the end of Fleecy Dale Road onto PA 32.

7.5 Arrive back at the Lumberville General Store and turn left onto the bridge that crosses back into New Jersey.
You'll see the towpath trail on your left, along the banks of the river. Continue from mile 16.0.

21

The Delaware's Paths and Trails

- **TOUR DISTANCE:** 33 miles (40 miles with Option)
- **TERRAIN:** Moderate, with rolling terrain for the first half of the ride; and easy, with flat terrain for the second half of the ride
- **SPECIAL FEATURES:** Washington Crossing State Park; Delaware Canal State Park; Bull's Island Recreation Area; Lumberville, Pennsylvania; New Hope, Pennsylvania; Lambertville, New Jersey

This ride starts in Mercer County, New Jersey, at Washington Crossing State Park, located beside the Delaware River. It was here that the Continental Army under the command of General George Washington landed after their historic crossing of the Delaware River on Christmas night in 1776. The site was chosen for a crossing because of a little-known ferry that was established here in about 1700. The battles that ensued between the Continental Army and the Hessian and British troops are often referred to by historians as the turning point of the Revolutionary War. The park has a museum and visitors center, an open-air theater, picnicking, and a nature center.

Leaving the park, the tour passes open meadows and farms and soon crosses into Hunterdon County. We pedal on Lower Creek Road, one of the most scenic lanes in New Jersey, and arrive at Bull's Island Recreation Area. The handsome footbridge crossing the Delaware River leads to Lumberville, Pennsylvania, where we discover the Black Bass Inn, whose history dates from 1740. More

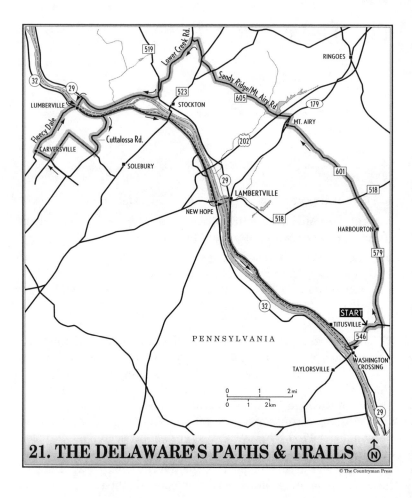

RINGOES

Lower Creek Rd.

Sandy Ridge/Mt. Airy Rd.

519

523

605

179

32

29

LUMBERVILLE

STOCKTON

MT. AIRY

Fleecy Dale

Cuttalossa Rd.

202

601

CARVERSVILLE

SOLEBURY

518

29

LAMBERTVILLE

NEW HOPE

518

HARBOURTON

579

32

START

TITUSVILLE

546

PENNSYLVANIA

WASHINGTON
CROSSING

TAYLORSVILLE

0   1   2 mi

0   1   2 km

29

21. THE DELAWARE'S PATHS & TRAILS

N

0.0	Turn right from Visitors Center parking area toward Washington Crossing State Park exit
0.3	Turn right to park exit
0.5	Turn left onto CR 546/Washington Crossing/Pennington Road
1.0	Turn left onto CR 579/Trenton-Harbourton Road
4.1	Turn left onto Harbourton–Mt. Airy Road
5.3	Go straight onto CR 601
8.6	Turn right onto Mt. Airy Village Road
9.0	Go across NJ 179 onto unmarked CR 605/Queen Road (becomes Sandy Ridge–Mt. Airy Road)
12.1	Turn left onto Sandy Ridge Road (unmarked)
	Turn right immediately onto Cemetery Road
12.6	Turn right onto CR 523/Stockton-Flemington Road
12.7	Turn left onto Covered Bridge Road
13.4	Turn left onto Lower Creek Road
15.4	Turn left onto CR 519 (unmarked)
15.5	Turn right onto NJ 29/River Road
18.3	Turn left into Bull's Island Recreation Area and cross bridge over the Delaware River to Lumberville, Pennsylvania; Option begins here
18.5	Turn right onto PA 32 on Pennsylvania side of the river
18.6	Turn right across small bridge onto Delaware Canal Towpath
21.8	Continue straight on towpath, passing bridge to Stockton Village
25.7	Turn left from path onto Bridge Street in New Hope and cross bridge back to Lambertville, New Jersey
26.0	Turn right onto Delaware and Raritan Canal Path in Lambertville
32.1	Turn left onto CR 546/Washington Crossing/Pennington Road
	Turn left immediately onto the overpass leading into Washington Crossing State Park
32.4	Turn right into Washington Crossing State Park
33.0	Turn right into Visitors Center parking area to end tour

Option (from mile 18.3)

0.0	Turn left onto PA 32
0.8	Turn right onto Cuttaloosa Road
2.3	Turn right onto Sugan Road
2.5	Turn right to continue on Sugan Road
3.5	Turn left onto Saw Mill Road
4.5	Turn right onto Aquetong Road
5.1	Arrive in Carversville
	Bear right onto Fleecy Dale Road
7.2	Turn right onto PA 32
7.4	Turn left across small bridge to Delaware Canal Towpath
	Turn right immediately onto path; continue from mile 18.5

historical information on Lumberville is included in tour 20, Flemington to Lumberville, Pennsylvania.

The return ride is on the Delaware Canal State Park Recreation Trail (DCSPR Trail), running alongside the river all the way to New Hope, Pennsylvania. The trail's surface is unpaved but has recently been improved and is quite suitable for a hybrid-type bicycle. Canoeing, rafting, and boating on the Delaware can be seen from the trail throughout the summer.

The DCSPR Trail is 60 miles in length and is the only remaining continuously intact canal from the great towpath and canal building era of the early and mid-19nth century. The U.S. Congress officially recognized the canal's importance to the economic evolution of America by establishing the Delaware and Lehigh Corridor and designating the canal as a registered National Historic Landmark.

The tour leaves the trail in the much visited and historic town of New Hope, Pennsylvania, which has long been a popular small-town escape from New York City. It's easy to spend some time browsing the many shops or walking across the bridge spanning the Delaware River to Lambertville, New Jersey. In Lambertville we can enjoy both the feel of a colonial village and the modern-day pastime of browsing in the many antiques shops here. Lambertville is also noted for its bed & breakfast lodging and fine dining. The cycling loop is completed with a flat, 6-mile pedal along the Delaware and Raritan Canal Trail in New Jersey, which leads back to Washington Crossing State Park.

DRIVING DIRECTIONS   Take the New Jersey Turnpike south to exit 14, I-78 west. Take I-78 west approximately 27 miles to I-287 south. Continue 3 miles to exit 17, US 202/US 206 toward Princeton and Somerville. Continue onto US 202 south toward Flemington. At Flemington continue around the traffic circle onto US 202/NJ 31 south. Travel 5.5 miles, turn right onto NJ 31 south, and continue 2.5 miles to CR 579. Turn right at the traffic light onto CR 579 and continue 6 miles to unmarked Washington Crossing Road. (The park office is on the left here.) Turn right at the traffic light to continue on Washington Crossing Road.

While the bridge across the Delaware from Bull's Island Recreation Area to Lumberville, Pennsylvania, can be traveled only by foot, this one spanning the river at Riegelsville can be used by both pedestrians and cars.

Continue approximately 0.5 mile and turn right into the park entrance. Turn left in the park toward the Visitors Center and take the first left after 0.3 mile into the Visitors Center parking area. There may be a seasonal $3 parking fee.

There are bathrooms inside the Visitors Center.

Drive time from New York City is 1 hour and 30 minutes.

RIDE DIRECTIONS

0.0 Turn right from the Visitors Center parking area at the yield sign toward the Washington Crossing State Park exit.

0.3 Turn right at the stop sign to exit the park.

0.5 Turn left onto CR 546/Washington Crossing Road/Pennington Road.

1.0 Turn left at the traffic light onto CR 579/Trenton-Harbourton Road.

4.1 Turn left onto Harbourton/Mt. Airy Road at the Village Store Historical Marker.
There's an old stone building here that was once the village store.

5.3 Go straight onto CR 601 north.

8.6 Turn right onto CR 601/Mt. Airy Village Road.

9.0 Cross NJ 179 onto unmarked CR 605/Queen Road (which becomes Sandy Ridge–Mt. Airy Road).
There's a sign on the opposite side of the road that reads LAMBERTVILLE COMPRESSOR STATION.

12.1 Turn left at the church onto unmarked Sandy Ridge Road.

Turn right immediately onto Cemetery Road.

12.6 Turn right at the end of Cemetery Road onto CR 523/Stockton-Flemington Road.

12.7 Take the first left onto Covered Bridge Road.
The downhill is winding here.

13.4 Turn left at the end of Covered Bridge Road onto Lower Creek Road.
This sun-dappled road that follows a stream is one of the most scenic in New Jersey.

15.4 Turn left at the end of Lower Creek Road onto unmarked CR 519.

15.5 Turn right at the end of CR 519 onto NJ 29 north/River Road.
A left turn here takes you first past the Prallsville Mill Site on the right, which is the Headquarters of the Delaware and Raritan State Park, and in 0.7 mile into the village of Stockton, where there are a number of lunch options.

18.3 Turn left into Bull's Island Recreation Area.
Look for the brown sign on the left and walk across the footbridge over the Delaware River into Lumberville, Pennsylvania. There are a number of lunch choices in Lumberville. The Option begins here.

18.5 Turn right onto PA 32 on the Pennsylvania side of the river.

18.6 Turn right across the small bridge onto the Delaware Canal Towpath, then turn right on the towpath to head south.

There are three low bridges on this path before it reaches New Hope. You'll have to dismount and walk your bike under each of them. The path follows the bank of the Delaware River, has a good riding surface, and is quite scenic.

21.8 Continue straight on the towpath, passing the bridge leading to Stockton Village.

25.7 Turn left from the path onto Bridge Street in New Hope.

You may stay in New Hope for lunch or walk across the bridge over the Delaware to New Jersey for lunch in Lambertville. New Hope is a historic village, while its sister town Lambertville is known for its antiques shops.

26.0 Turn right onto the Delaware and Raritan Canal Path in Lambertville, just past the Inn at Lambertville Station Restaurant.

32.1 Leaving the towpath, turn left onto CR 546/Washington Crossing Road/Pennington Road.

Turn left immediately onto the overpass leading into Washington Crossing State Park.

There's a bridge to Pennsylvania on the right and a small store to the left here.

32.4 Turn right onto the paved road into Washington Crossing State Park.

33.0 Turn right into the Visitors Center parking area to end the tour.

Option

0.0 From mile 18.3 turn left onto PA 32 south, cycling through Lumberville, Pennsylvania.

0.8 Turn right onto Cuttaloosa Road.

This road leads uphill, passing Cuttaloosa Farm, where there are often farm animals on either side of the road. The setting here is quite lovely and reminiscent of the English countryside. The road here is unpaved for about 0.7 mile.

2.3 Turn right onto Sugan Road.

2.5 Turn right to continue on Sugan Road.

3.5 Turn left onto Saw Mill Road at the NO OUTLET sign.

4.5 Turn right onto Aquetong Road.
This road continues into the hamlet of Carversville, where there's a general store on the right.

5.1 Arrive in Carversville and bear right onto Fleecy Dale Road at the Carversville General Store.
Fleecy Dale Road follows a small river and is one of the most picturesque roads in Pennsylvania, with many old stone buildings along it.

7.2 Turn right onto PA 32.

7.4 Turn left across the small bridge to the Delaware Canal Towpath.

Turn right immediately onto the towpath.
Continue from mile 18.5.

22

Turkey Swamp to Allentown

- **TOUR DISTANCE:** 45 miles
- **TERRAIN:** Easy, with gentle terrain
- **SPECIAL FEATURES:** Turkey Swamp Park, Allentown

Monmouth County's eastern border is on the ocean, and much of the terrain here is quite gentle, offering many opportunities for effortless cycling along secondary roads. Turkey Swamp Park is located in a unique wooded setting at the center of the county and offers camping, hiking, canoeing, boating, and fishing on its 17-acre lake.

Exiting the parking area, the road is unpaved for 0.2 mile, but after this paved roads lead cyclists along an easy course that passes small farms bordering either side of the road. The tour continues through the Assunpink Wildlife Management Area on the way to Allentown. The Assunpink is a 5,600-acre area of fields, hedgerows, and lakes that remains dedicated to the preservation and viewing of wildlife and is considered one of the best areas for bird-watching in New Jersey. Approximately one thousand acres of land are farmed by a handful of farmers who, in exchange for their leases, have to leave 15 percent of their crops standing for animals to forage. Stop for a moment to admire an attractive horse farm as the route exits the wildlife area.

Allentown's Main Street has been restored in the past few years, but it remains a town steeped in Revolutionary War history. The battle for the stone bridge in Allentown during the War of Independence is reenacted each year in late June by the Road to

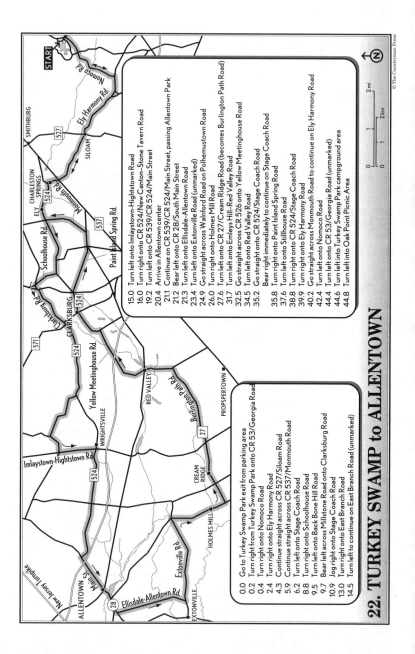

22. TURKEY SWAMP to ALLENTOWN

0.0   Go to Turkey Swamp Park exit from parking area
0.2   Turn right from Turkey Swamp Park onto CR 53/Georgia Road
0.4   Turn right onto Nomoco Road
2.4   Turn right onto Ely Harmony Road
4.3   Continue straight across CR 527/Siloam Road
5.9   Continue straight across CR 537/Monmouth Road
6.2   Turn left onto Stage Coach Road
8.8   Turn right onto Schoolhouse Road
9.5   Turn left onto Back Bone Hill Road
9.7   Bear left across Millstone Road onto Clarksburg Road
10.9 Jog right onto Stage Coach Road
13.0 Turn right onto East Branch Road
14.5 Turn left to continue on East Branch Road (unmarked)

15.0 Turn left onto Imlaystown-Hightstown Road
16.0 Turn right onto CR 524/New Canton–Stone Tavern Road
19.2 Turn left onto CR 539/CR 524/Main Street
20.4 Arrive in Allentown center
21.1 Continue on CR 539/CR 524/Main Street, passing Allentown Park
21.2 Bear left onto CR 28/South Main Street
21.3 Turn left onto Ellisdale-Allentown Road
23.4 Turn left onto Extonville Road (unmarked)
24.9 Go straight across Walnford Road on Polhemustown Road
26.0 Turn right onto Holmes Mill Road
27.6 Turn left onto CR 27/Cream Ridge Road (becomes Burlington Path Road)
31.7 Turn left onto Emleys Hill–Red Valley Road
32.5 Go straight across CR 526 onto Yellow Meetinghouse Road
34.5 Turn left onto Red Valley Road
35.2 Go straight onto CR 524/Stage Coach Road
      Bear right immediately to continue on Stage Coach Road
35.8 Turn right onto Paint Island Spring Road
37.6 Turn left onto Stillhouse Road
38.8 Turn right onto CR 524/Stage Coach Road
39.9 Turn right onto Ely Harmony Road
40.2 Go straight across Monmouth Road to continue on Ely Harmony Road
42.4 Turn left onto Nomoco Road
44.4 Turn left onto CR 53/Georgia Road (unmarked)
44.6 Turn left into Turkey Swamp Park campground area
44.8 Turn left into Oak Point Picnic Area

© The Countryman Press

Monmouth Heritage Campaign. A wonderful option is purchasing lunch at Woody's Diner and sitting on a bench in the park beside the pond just 0.2 mile south on Main Street. If time allows, there are antiques shops for browsing just across from the park.

After lunch the route crosses Walnford Road 4 miles outside of Allentown. Historic Walnford Village is just 0.4 mile off the route and is worth a visit. The history of Walnford Village is described in tour 23, Allentown with a Twist.

Between Burlington Path Road and the intersection of Stage Coach Road—about 9 miles—the cycling is quite special: The road here is framed by woodlands, meadows, and striking horse farms.

DRIVING DIRECTIONS   Take the New Jersey Turnpike south to exit 8. Bear right onto NJ 33 east for 6.5 miles. Turn right onto CR 527A for about 2 miles. At the stop sign continue straight onto CR 527 south. Turn left after 3.8 miles onto Ely Harmony Road. Continue for 2 miles and turn left onto Nomoco Road. Continue for 2 miles and turn left at the end of Nomoco Road onto CR 53/ Georgia Road. Turn left immediately into the campground in Turkey Swamp Park. After 0.2 mile turn left into the Oak Point picnic area and Camp Office parking area.

There are bathrooms to the right on the outside of the office building.

Drive time from New York City is 1 hour and 15 minutes.

RIDE DIRECTIONS

0.0 Leave the parking area and go to the Turkey Swamp Park exit.

0.2 Turn right from Turkey Swamp Park onto CR 53/Georgia Road.

0.4 Take the first right onto Nomoco Road.

2.4 Turn right at the end of Nomoco Road onto Ely Harmony Road.

4.3 Cross CR 527/Siloam Road to continue on Ely Harmony Road.

5.9 Go straight across CR 537/Monmouth Road to continue on Ely Harmony Road.
There's a small deli on the right just after Monmouth Road.

6.2 Turn left at the end of Ely Harmony Road onto Stage Coach Road.

8.8 Turn right onto Schoolhouse Road.
This turn is easy to miss because the signpost is on the left. The route becomes rolling here for 2 miles.

9.5 Turn left onto Back Bone Hill Road.

9.7 Jog left across Millstone Road onto Clarksburg Road.

10.9 Bear right onto Stage Coach Road at the stop sign.
To extend this ride 8.5 miles, after 0.1 mile on Stage Coach Road, turn right toward the Borough of Roosevelt. Follow CR 571 north for 2.3 miles and then turn right onto South Rochdale Road for 2.2 miles to the post office building. The history of Roosevelt is described in more detail in tour 23, Allentown with a Twist. Reverse direction to return to the main ride at this mile point.

13.0 Turn right onto East Branch Road toward Assunpink.
The ride passes through part of the Assunpink Wildlife Management Area.

Good family fun!

14.5 Turn left to continue on unmarked East Branch Road.
Note the attractive horse farm upon leaving the Assunpink Wildlife Management Area.

15.0 Turn left onto Imlayston-Hightstown Road.

16.0 Turn right onto CR 524/New Canton–Stone Tavern Road.

19.2 Turn left onto CR 539/CR 524/Main Street in Allentown.

20.4 Arrive in Allentown center for lunch.
Woody's Restaurant, just past the intersection of CR 526 and Church Street, is the best bet for either a full-service lunch or a take-out sandwich to enjoy in the park 0.2 mile farther down the road on the left.

21.1 To leave Allentown, continue south on CR 539/CR 524/Main Street.

21.2 Bear left onto CR 28/South Main Street.

21.3 Turn left onto Ellisdale-Allentown Road.

23.4 Turn left at the end of Ellisdale-Allendale Road onto unmarked Extonville Road.

24.9 Go straight across Walnford Road onto Polhemustown Road.
Historic Walnford Village is 0.4 mile to the right on Walnford Road.

26.0 Turn right onto Holmes Mill Road.

27.6 Turn left onto CR 27/Cream Ridge Road (which becomes Burlington Path Road).
The ride begins to follow a ridge here, offering pastoral views of the countryside with an exceptionally lovely horse farm just at the turn onto Red Valley Road.

31.7 Turn left at the boarded-up house onto Emleys Hill–Red Valley Road.

32.5 Go straight across CR 526 onto Yellow Meetinghouse Road.

34.5 Turn left at the end of Yellow Meeting House Road onto Red Valley Road.

35.2 Go straight at the stop sign onto CR 524/Stage Coach Road.

Bear right immediately at Clarksburg General Store to continue on Stage Coach Road.
A bathroom is available at the store.

35.8 Turn right onto Paint Island Spring Road at the John Deere sign. *At this intersection take care not to take the hard right turn.*

37.6 Turn left onto Stillhouse Road.

38.8 Turn right onto CR 524/Stage Coach Road.

39.9 Turn right onto Ely Harmony Road.

40.2 Go straight across Monmouth Road on Ely Harmony Road.

42.4 Turn left onto Nomoco Road.

44.4 Turn left at the end of Nomoco Road onto unmarked CR 53/Georgia Road.

44.6 Take the first left into the Turkey Swamp Park campground area.

44.8 Turn left into the Oak Point picnic area.
If you have time at the end of the ride, take the opportunity to visit the lake at Turkey Swamp Park, just behind the ranger's building alongside the parking area.

23

Allentown with a Twist

- **TOUR DISTANCE:** 41 miles (50 miles with Option)
- **TERRAIN:** Easy, with flat and gently rolling terrain
- **SPECIAL FEATURES:** Allentown, Crosswicks Village, Historic Walnford Village

On this easy ride we freewheel along Monmouth County's country roads, passing open meadows, planted fields, and attractive horse farms. The directions are organized in a figure eight, which brings us back through Allentown after the morning loop and again after the afternoon ride.

After leaving Allentown in the morning we pass through the Assunpink Wildlife Management Area, which encompasses 5,600 acres of fields, hedgerows, and woods that typify the vegetation of much of central New Jersey. This area remains dedicated to the preservation and viewing of wildlife and is considered one of the best areas for bird-watching in the state. In the morning ride an 8-mile out-and-back to the Borough of Roosevelt is included primarily for its historical significance. The cooperative called the Jersey Homesteads opened in 1936 with the assistance of FDR's New Deal subsistence program. The federal government granted $500,000 for the creation of a unique community of two hundred Bauhaus cinderblock, flat-roofed, bungalow-type houses. Individual homesteaders were to provide an additional $500 for the construction of their homes. The bungalows, some of which still exist in their original form, attracted members of the garment workers

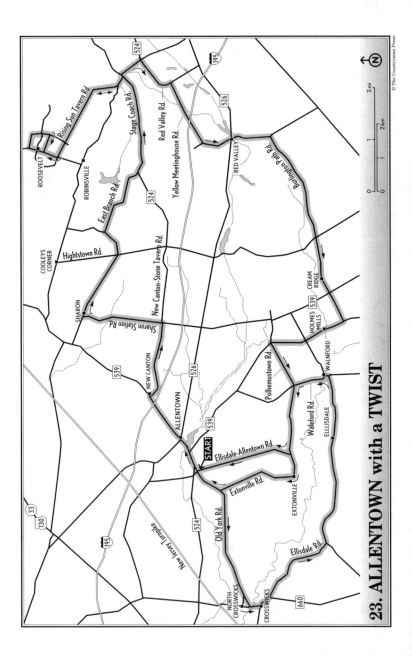

23. ALLENTOWN with a TWIST

0.0 Turn right from Byron Johnson Park parking area onto Ellisdale-Allentown Road
0.1 Turn right immediately onto CR 28/South Main Street
0.2 Go straight onto South Main Street into Allentown
0.5 Go straight onto CR 524/CR 539/Main Street through Allentown
0.8 Go straight onto North Main Street to leave Allentown
1.9 Go across I-95/CR 524 and turn right onto CR 524/New Canton-Stone Tavern Road
3.5 Turn left onto Sharon Station Road
5.1 Turn right onto Sharon Station–East Branch Road (unmarked)
6.6 Go straight across Hightstown Road to continue on Sharon Station–East Branch Road
7.1 Turn right onto East Branch Road
8.7 Turn left onto CR524/Stage Coach Road
10.8 Bear right onto CR 524/CR 571; Option begins just before turn
11.2 Turn right onto Red Valley Road
12.1 Turn right onto Yellow Meetinghouse Road
14.2 Go straight onto Emleys Hill–Red Valley Road
15.0 Turn left onto Burlington Path Road
18.4 Go straight onto CR27/Cream Ridge Road
19.1 Turn right onto Holmes Mill Road
20.7 Turn left onto Polhemustown Road
21.7 Go straight across Walnford Road onto Extonville Road
23.2 Go straight to continue on Extonville Road, passing Province Line Road on the left
23.6 Turn right to continue on Extonville Road
25.2 Turn right onto CR 28/Old York Road (becomes Allentown-Crosswicks Road)
26.0 Go straight onto South Main Street
26.3 Continue on CR 524/CR 539 toward Allentown
26.5 Arrive in Allentown
     Reverse direction to leave Allentown on CR 524/CR 539/South Main Street
26.7 Go straight onto CR 524
27.0 Go straight onto CR 28/Old York Road (becomes Allentown-Crosswicks Road)
30.3 Turn left onto Church Street at the end of Allentown-Crosswicks Road
30.6 Turn left onto CR 660/Main Street in Crosswicks
30.8 Go straight onto Ellisdale Road at intersection with Chesterfield-Crosswicks Road
37.1 Turn left onto Walnford Road
37.2 Pass Walnford Village on the right
37.9 Turn left onto Extonville Road
39.3 Turn right onto Ellisdale-Allentown Road (unmarked)
41.3 Turn right into Byron Johnson Park parking area to end tour

     Option (from mile 10.8)
0.0 Turn left onto CR 571/Tavern Road (becomes Rising Sun Road just before turn at mile 10.8)
2.3 Turn right onto South Rochdale Road
4.5 Pass Roosevelt Post Office and turn right onto Farm Lane
4.9 Turn left onto North Valley Road
5.3 Turn left onto Oscar Lane
5.6 Turn left onto South Rochdale Road (unmarked)
6.2 Turn left onto CR 571/Clarksburg Road/Rising Sun Road
8.5 Turn left onto CR 524/CR 571 and continue from mile 10.8

industry who went on to establish a modern working factory here. The original Tripod Coat and Suit Company now houses a manufacturer of packaging machinery. The cooperative community also attracted an impressive group of painters and photographers such as Ben Shahan, who assisted Diego Rivera on murals created for Rockefeller Center.

The cycling in the first half of the tour is bordered by pastoral views of the countryside leading back to Allentown. Once in Allentown, a good plan for lunch is a picnic in the park beside a pond, just 0.2 mile south of the main intersection in the center of town. If time allows, there are antiques shops for browsing just across from the park.

The afternoon loop continues into Burlington County and passes through the village of Crosswicks. Many of the homes both here and in Allentown are vintage 18th century with Revolutionary War history. The skirmishes that took place in both villages with the Queen's Rangers, who were American loyalists to the king of England, are reenacted each year in late June by the Road to Monmouth Heritage Campaign. Recrossing county lines, the route passes Historic Walnford Village, which was founded in 1734 on a 180-acre plantation and included one of the many gristmills in the area. As the property was developed, it eventually included a sawmill, blacksmith shop, copper shop, both private and tenant homes, orchards, and one hundred plowed acres. The site is open daily for touring; however, the gristmill is open only on weekends from April through November.

DRIVING DIRECTIONS   Take the New Jersey Turnpike south to exit 7A. Continue onto I-195 east and take exit 8 onto CR 524 west into Allentown. Turn right from the exit and continue onto South Main Street, which is also CR 526/CR 539. After 0.3 mile continue straight onto CR 524 west. After 0.2 mile continue straight onto NJ 28. After 0.2 mile turn left onto Ellisdale Road and then turn left immediately into the parking area of Byron Johnson Park.

There are bathrooms at the parking area.

Drive time from New York City is 1 hour and 20 minutes.

RIDE DIRECTIONS

0.0 Turn right from Byron Johnson Park parking area onto Ellisdale-Allentown Road.

0.1 Turn right immediately onto CR 28/South Main Street.

0.2 Go straight onto South Main Street into Allentown.

0.5 Go straight onto CR 524 east/CR 539/Main Street in Allentown.
You'll be cycling through Allentown's center, passing the pond on the right side of the road that's the perfect spot for a picnic lunch after the morning's ride.

0.8 Go straight onto North Main Street to leave Allentown.

1.9 Go across CR 195 and turn right onto CR 524/New Canton–Stone Tavern Road.

3.5 Turn left onto Sharon Station Road.

5.1 Turn right at the stop sign at the end of Sharon Station Road onto unmarked Sharon Station–East Branch Road.

6.6 Go straight across Hightstown Road to continue on Sharon Station–East Branch Road.
Note the attractive horse farm just before entering the Assunpink Wildlife Management Area.

7.1 Turn right onto East Branch Road.

8.7 Turn left at the stop sign at the end of East Branch Road onto NJ 524/Stage Coach Road.

10.7 Turn left for Option to Roosevelt.

10.8 Bear right onto CR 524/CR 571.

11.2 Turn right onto Red Valley Road.
The Clarksburg General Store is on the left here and is a good place to purchase a drink. They also have a bathroom.

12.1 Take the first right onto Yellow Meetinghouse Road.

14.2 Go straight onto Emleys Hill–Red Valley Road.

The countryside here and all along Burlington Path Road is particularly eye-catching; there are many attractive horse farms and open meadows along the road.

15.0 Turn right at the stop sign at the end of Emleys Hill–Red Valley Road onto Burlington Path Road.

18.4 Go straight at the stop sign onto CR 27/Cream Ridge Road.

19.1 Turn right at the stop sign at the end of CR 27/Cream Ridge Road onto Holmes Mill Road.

20.7 Make a hard left onto Polhemustown Road at the stop sign.

21.7 Go straight across Walnford Road onto Extonville Road.
There's a very large tree nursery here just before the route continues straight past Province Line Road.

23.2 Go straight to continue on Extonville Road, passing Province Line Road on the left.

23.6 Turn right to continue on Extonville Road.

25.2 Turn right at the stop sign onto CR 28/Old York Road (which becomes Allentown-Crosswicks Road).

26.0 Go straight onto South Main Street.

26.3 Continue straight on CR 524 east/CR 539 north toward Allentown.

26.5 Arrive in Allentown.
Woody's Restaurant is a good place to purchase a sandwich for a picnic lunch. It's only 0.2 mile from the park on Main Street.

Leave Allentown on CR 524 south/CR 539 south/South Main Street.

26.7 Go straight onto CR 524.

27.0 Go straight onto CR 28/Old York Road (which becomes Allentown-Crosswicks Road).

30.3 Turn left onto Church Street at the end of Allentown-Crosswicks Road.

30.6 Turn left onto CR 660/Main Street in Crosswicks.
Take some time to explore Crosswicks Village.

A nice, flat straightaway

30.8 Go straight onto Ellisdale Road at the intersection with Chesterfield-Crosswicks Road.

37.1 Turn left onto Walnford Road.

37.2 Pass Historic Walnford Village on the right.
If you have time and it's open, the gristmill makes for an interesting visit. There are portable bathrooms near the parking area.

37.9 Turn left onto Extonville Road.

39.3 Turn right onto unmarked Ellisdale-Allentown Road.

41.3 Turn right into the Byron Johnson Park parking area to end the tour.

Option

0.0 From mile 10.7 turn left onto CR 571/Tavern Road (which becomes Rising Sun Road just before the turn at mile 10.8).

2.3 Turn right onto South Rochdale Road.

Arrive at the Roosevelt Post Office and walk across the street to the park, where there is a low brick wall with a sculpted bust paying homage to FDR for his role in creating the cooperative community of Roosevelt. The artist is Jon Shahan, son of the famous artist Ben Shahan, who has a famous mural in the elementary school beside the park. If someone is in the school, he or she may let you take a look at the mural.

4.5 Turn right onto Farm Lane just past the post office.

Note some of the original 1936 bungalows on either side of the road.

4.9 Turn left onto North Valley Road.

5.3 Turn left onto Oscar Lane.

The original garment workers factory building sits at the corner of North Valley Road and Oscar Drive.

5.6 Turn left at the end of Oscar Lane onto unmarked South Rochdale Road.

6.2 Turn left onto CR 571 south/Clarksburg Road/Rising Sun Road.

8.5 Turn left onto CR 524/CR 571 south.

Continue from mile 10.8.

24

Three Counties

- **TOUR DISTANCE:** 39 miles (44 miles with Option)
- **TERRAIN:** Easy, with rolling terrain in the second half of the tour
- **SPECIAL FEATURES:** Historic Walnford Village, Allentown

This tour is an easy ride across three of central New Jersey's counties. Here cyclists glide by farmland and through a landscape that is an integral part of our Revolutionary War history.

We start pedaling from a small park in Bordentown, Burlington County, and continue over fairly flat terrain for 12 miles. Bordentown played an important role in the Revolutionary War and was occupied by British and German troops no less than three times. During the second occupation in January 1777, Colonel Borden of the Burlington County Militia constructed floating mines at his local copper shop on Park Street. The mines, referred to as kegs, were floated down the Delaware River toward Philadelphia, where the British fleet was anchored. One of the kegs struck a British barge, killing four men. This event was later referred to as the Battle of the Kegs and was made famous in a poem by Francis Hopkinson.

The route continues through Cookstown, where the flat terrain leads past a signpost welcoming all to Ocean County. After a few turns of the pedals cyclists arrive at the village of New Egypt, which is at the geographical center of New Jersey. A sandwich from Scott's Market to the right on Main Street makes a perfect lunch,

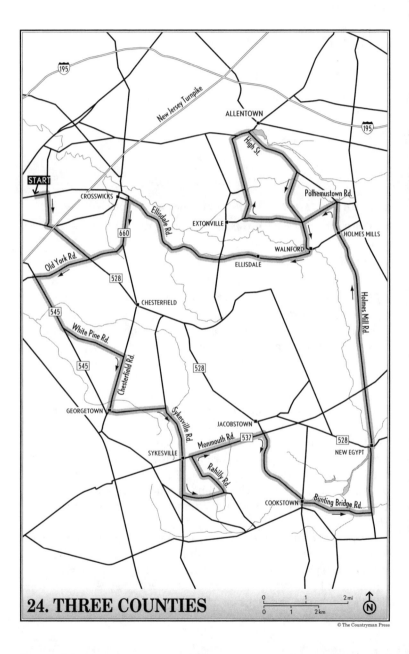

24. THREE COUNTIES

START

I-195

New Jersey Turnpike

ALLENTOWN

High St.

Polhemustown Rd.

CROSSWICKS

Ellisdale Rd.

EXTONVILLE

HOLMES MILLS

660

WALNFORD

Old York Rd.

528

ELLISDALE

545

CHESTERFIELD

Holmes Mill Rd.

White Pine Rd.

545

Chesterfield Rd.

528

GEORGETOWN

Sykesville Rd.

JACOBSTOWN

528

Monmouth Rd. 537

NEW EGYPT

SYKESVILLE

Rahilly Rd.

COOKSTOWN

Bunting Bridge Rd.

0   1   2 mi

0   1   2 km

N

© The Countryman Press

0.0 Turn right from Lawrence Park onto Ward Avenue
0.3 Turn right onto Hogback Road
1.0 Turn left onto CR 528/Bordentown-Chesterfield Road
2.3 Turn right onto CR 660/Old York Road
3.8 Turn left onto CR 545/Bordentown-Georgetown Road
5.1 Turn left onto White Pine Road
6.8 Turn right onto Chesterfield Road
8.1 Turn left onto Georgetown Road (becomes Herman Black Road)
9.5 Turn right onto Sykesville Road
10.8 Go straight across CR 537/Monmouth Road to continue on Sykesville Road
11.7 Turn left onto CR 668/Croshaw Road
12.7 Turn left onto Rahilly Road
14.0 Turn right onto CR 537/Monmouth Road
15.9 Turn right onto CR 665/Jacobstown-Cookstown Road
18.0 Turn right onto Cookstown Road/Main Street
     Turn left immediately onto Bunting Bridge Road
19.8 Turn left onto Brindletown Road (becomes Mill Street)
21.3 Turn right onto Main Street in New Egypt
     Turn left immediately onto Evergreen Road (becomes Holmes Mill Road)
22.6 Go straight across CR 537 onto CR 27/Holmes Mill Road
27.1 Make a hard left turn onto Polhemustown Road
28.2 Turn left onto Walnford Road; Option begins here
28.8 Pass Walnford Village on left
28.9 Turn right onto Hill Road (becomes Ellisdale Road)
30.3 Go straight across Extonville Road to continue on Ellisdale Road
34.3 Turn left onto CR 660/Chesterfield-Crosswicks Road
35.4 Bear right onto Old York Road
36.3 Turn right onto CR 528/Bordentown-Chesterfield Road
37.7 Turn right onto Hogback Road
38.4 Turn left onto Ward Avenue
38.7 End at Lawrence Park

Option (from mile 28.2)
0.0 Go straight across Walnford Road on Extonville Road (unmarked)
1.5 Turn right onto Ellisdale-Allentown Road
3.6 Turn right onto CR 28/Old York Road (becomes Main Street)
4.0 Turn right onto CR 539/High Street in Allentown
5.6 Turn right onto Walns Mill Road
7.0 Go straight across Polhemustown Road onto Walnford Road. Continue from mile 28.8

or for those who may want a sit-down lunch, the Plum Street Restaurant is to the left, 0.2 mile down Main Street, on the right side of the road.

Shortly after leaving New Egypt the route crosses over county lines once again, this time into Monmouth County. Historic Walnford Village is worth a stop, especially on weekends when the old gristmill is open for touring. The village was founded in 1734 on a 180-acre plantation and included one of the many gristmills in the area. Just before turning toward Walnford Village there's a 7-mile Option that loops toward Allentown and returns, passing the village. There are a few short climbs after Walnford Village on the way to Crosswicks, but the scenery is eye-catching here, with horse farms and lovely country homes along the route. Crosswicks played a role in the War of Independence, and the battle for the bridge at Crosswicks Creek is reenacted each year in late June by the Road to Monmouth Heritage Campaign. The last county line is crossed as the ride heads back into Burlington County and Bordentown.

DRIVING DIRECTIONS   Take the New Jersey Turnpike south to exit 7A. Take I-195 west to exit 5A and continue onto US 130 south. Travel for 5 miles on US 130 south and merge with US 206 south. Continue 0.6 mile on US 206 south. Just after the traffic light at Crosswicks Street, turn right onto Crosswicks Street and then make a left at the traffic light onto US 206 north. Continue 0.5 mile to Ward Avenue. The Town and Country Diner is on the corner here. Turn right onto Ward Avenue and continue 0.6 mile to the Lawrence Park parking area.

There is a bathroom at Lawrence Park, but if it's closed the Town and Country Diner has bathroom facilities.

Drive time from New York City is 1 hour and 20 minutes.

RIDE DIRECTIONS

0.0 Leaving Lawrence Park, turn right onto Ward Avenue.

0.3 Turn right onto Hogback Road.

1.0 Turn left onto CR 528/Bordentown–Chesterfield Road.

2.3 Turn right onto CR 660/Old York Road.

3.8 Turn left at the stop sign onto CR 545 south/Bordentown-Georgetown Road.

5.1 Turn left onto White Pine Road.
The signpost for this turn is on the left and is easy to miss.

6.8 Turn right at the stop sign at the end of White Pine Road onto Chesterfield Road.

8.1 Turn left onto Georgetown Road (which becomes Herman Black Road).

9.5 Turn right at the stop sign at the end of Georgetown Road onto Sykesville Road.

10.8 Go straight across CR 537/Monmouth Road to continue on Sykesville Road.

11.7 Turn left onto CR 668/Croshaw Road.

12.7 Turn left onto Rahilly Road.

14.0 Turn right at the stop sign at the end of Rahilly Road onto CR 537/Monmouth Road.
There's fast-moving traffic here for 2 miles, but the road has an adequate shoulder.

15.9 Turn right at the first flashing light onto CR 665/Jacobstown-Cookstown Road.

18.0 Turn right at the stop sign at the end of Jacobstown-Cookstown Road onto Cookstown Road/Main Street.

Turn left immediately onto Bunting Bridge Road.
This turn occurs just past the Cookstown General Store.

19.8 Turn left at the stop sign at the end of Cookstown Road onto Brindletown Road (becomes Mill Street).

21.3 Turn right onto Main Street in New Egypt.
The Plum Street Restaurant is located to the left on Main Street, and Scott's Market is located on the right.

To leave New Egypt, turn left just before Scott's Market onto Evergreen Road (becomes Holmes Mill Road).

22.6 Go straight across CR 537 onto CR 27/Holmes Mill Road.
The route passes Walnford Road on the left.

27.1 Make a hard left turn onto Polhemustown Road.
Take care not to make the easy left onto busy CR 539.

28.2 Turn left onto Walnford Road.
The Option continues straight here.

28.8 Pass Historic Walnford Village on the left, just before the bridge.
It's worth a visit, especially if the gristmill is open for tours.

28.9 Turn right at the end of Walnford Road onto Hill Road (which becomes Ellisdale Road).
The countryside from here to Crosswicks has a few hills but is quite scenic, with horse farms and open meadows on either side of the road.

30.3 Go straight across Extonville Road to continue on Ellisdale Road.

34.3 Turn left at the stop sign onto CR 660/Chesterfield-Crosswicks Road.
The village of Crosswicks, just past the stop sign, is worth exploring.

35.4 Bear right onto Old York Road.

36.3 Turn right at the stop sign onto CR 528 west/Bordentown-Chesterfield Road.

37.7 Turn right onto Hogback Road after crossing the highway overpass.

38.4 Turn left onto Ward Avenue.

38.7 Turn left into Lawrence Park to end the tour.

Option

0.0 From mile 28.2 go straight across Walnford Road on unmarked Extonville Road.

1.5 Turn right onto Ellisdale-Allentown Road.

3.6 Turn right onto CR 28/Old York Road (which becomes Main Street).

4.0 Turn right onto CR 539/High Street in Allentown.
Continuing straight here for 0.3 mile will lead you into Allentown center.

5.6 Turn right onto Walns Mill Road.

7.0 Go straight across Polhemustown Road onto Walnford Road.
Continue from mile 28.8.

PENNSYLVANIA

25

Bucks County

- **TOUR DISTANCE:** 39 miles
- **TERRAIN:** Moderate to more difficult. This ride has it all: rolling terrain; flat, easy cycling; and a few very steep climbs.
- **SPECIAL FEATURES:** Bull's Island Recreation Area, Lumberville, Carversville, covered bridges of Bucks County, Pearl S. Buck Home

This ride begins on the New Jersey side of the Delaware River at Bull's Island Recreation Area, a 24-acre forested island with 69 tent and trailer campsites. From here cyclists walk across an attractive footbridge leading to the village of Lumberville in Bucks County, Pennsylvania.

Bucks County is one of the three original counties in Pennsylvania and was founded by William Penn in 1682. The early struggles for freedom and independence are now preserved in wonderfully maintained stone homes, old village churches, and covered bridges.

The cycling begins along the Delaware River and quickly leads to Fleecy Dale Road, one of the most attractive lanes in Bucks County. The setting along the Paunacussing Creek is a sun-dappled road lined with wonderful stone homes. Shortly the route passes through the center of the village of Carversville, listed on the National Register of Historic Places. There's a steep climb out of Carversville followed by a descent into a pretty dell-like setting where the tour continues through a covered bridge. The riding crosses into Dublin Borough, where the cycling becomes easier as the route flattens and passes farms and woodlands. Shopping for lunch in Dublin Village is wise because there are no services from here to the picnic spot on Lake Galena. The picnic area is delightfully situated along the lake in Peace Valley Park. Here there are 14 miles of nature trails at the eastern end of the lake, offering walking options that vary from groomed footpaths to remote hiking trails through mature woodlands.

Soon after a climb away from the lake, the route passes by the home of Peal S. Buck, writer of *The Good Earth* and the first woman to win both the Pulitzer and Nobel Prizes for literature. The home is a National Historic Landmark and has a unique blend of Chinese and 19th-century Pennsylvania art and architecture. Gentle terrain guides cyclists back to the Delaware River, where the ride passes through yet another covered bridge. The route then loops back through Carversville and onto Fleecy Dale Road, returning to the banks of the Delaware River. Take some time to explore the historic village of Lumberville and enjoy stopping into the Lumberville General Store for a refreshing drink. Lumberville's and Carversville's history are described in more detail in tour 20, Flemington to Lumberville, Pennsylvania. The cycling finishes in Lumberville, and all that's left to do is to walk back across the footbridge to Bull's Island Recreation Area in New Jersey.

DRIVING DIRECTIONS   Take the New Jersey Turnpike south to exit 14, I-78. Take I-78 west approximately 27 miles to I-287 south. Continue approximately 3 miles to exit 17, NJ 202/US 206. Continue on NJ 202 south toward Flemington. Continue on NJ 202 around the traffic circle in Flemington. Exit on NJ 202 south at the last exit in New Jersey. Turn left at the end of the exit ramp, then turn right onto NJ 29 toward Stockton. Continue past the village of Stockton about 2.5 miles to the Bull's Island Recreation Area at Raven Rock. Turn left into the Bull's Island Recreation Area and cross the small bridge to the second parking area.

Bathrooms are located beside the parking area for the Bull's Island Recreation Area.

Drive time from New York City is 1 hour and 30 minutes.

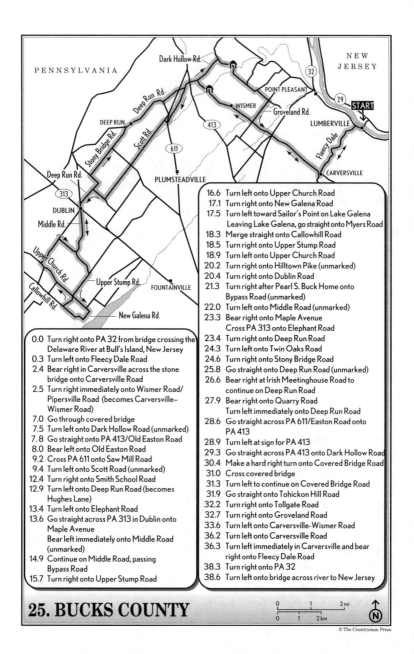

PENNSYLVANIA

Dark Hollow Rd.

NEW JERSEY

32

POINT PLEASANT

WISMER   Groveland Rd.

29   START

Deep Run Rd.

DEEP RUN

Stony Bridge Rd.

Scott Rd.

413

611

LUMBERVILLE

Fleecy Dale

Deep Run Rd.

313

PLUMSTEADVILLE

CARVERSVILLE

DUBLIN

Middle Rd.

Upper Church Rd.

Upper Stump Rd.

FOUNTAINVILLE

Callowhill Rd.

New Galena Rd.

0.0 Turn right onto PA 32 from bridge crossing the
     Delaware River at Bull's Island, New Jersey
0.3 Turn left onto Fleecy Dale Road
2.4 Bear right in Carversville across the stone
     bridge onto Carversville Road
2.5 Turn right immediately onto Wismer Road/
     Pipersville Road (becomes Carversville–
     Wismer Road)
7.0 Go through covered bridge
7.5 Turn left onto Dark Hollow Road (unmarked)
7.8 Go straight onto PA 413/Old Easton Road
8.0 Bear left onto Old Easton Road
9.2 Cross PA 611 onto Saw Mill Road
9.4 Turn left onto Scott Road (unmarked)
12.4 Turn right onto Smith School Road
12.9 Turn left onto Deep Run Road (becomes
     Hughes Lane)
13.4 Turn left onto Elephant Road
13.6 Go straight across PA 313 in Dublin onto
     Maple Avenue
     Bear left immediately onto Middle Road
     (unmarked)
14.9 Continue on Middle Road, passing
     Bypass Road
15.7 Turn right onto Upper Stump Road

16.6 Turn left onto Upper Church Road
17.1 Turn right onto New Galena Road
17.5 Turn left toward Sailor's Point on Lake Galena
     Leaving Lake Galena, go straight onto Myers Road
18.3 Merge straight onto Callowhill Road
18.5 Turn right onto Upper Stump Road
18.9 Turn left onto Upper Church Road
20.2 Turn right onto Hilltown Pike (unmarked)
20.4 Turn right onto Dublin Road
21.3 Turn right after Pearl S. Buck Home onto
     Bypass Road (unmarked)
22.0 Turn left onto Middle Road (unmarked)
23.3 Bear right onto Maple Avenue
     Cross PA 313 onto Elephant Road
23.4 Turn right onto Deep Run Road
24.3 Turn left onto Twin Oaks Road
24.6 Turn right onto Stony Bridge Road
25.8 Go straight onto Deep Run Road (unmarked)
26.6 Bear right at Irish Meetinghouse Road to
     continue on Deep Run Road
27.9 Bear right onto Quarry Road
     Turn left immediately onto Deep Run Road
28.6 Go straight across PA 611/Easton Road onto
     PA 413
28.9 Turn left at sign for PA 413
29.3 Go straight across PA 413 onto Dark Hollow Road
30.4 Make a hard right turn onto Covered Bridge Road
31.0 Cross covered bridge
31.3 Turn left to continue on Covered Bridge Road
31.9 Go straight onto Tohickon Hill Road
32.2 Turn right onto Tollgate Road
32.7 Turn right onto Groveland Road
33.6 Turn left onto Carversville-Wismer Road
36.2 Turn left onto Carversville Road
36.3 Turn left immediately in Carversville and bear
     right onto Fleecy Dale Road
38.3 Turn right onto PA 32
38.6 Turn left onto bridge across river to New Jersey

25. BUCKS COUNTY

0   1   2 mi
0   1   2 km

N

© The Countryman Press

RIDE DIRECTIONS

0.0 Leave the Bull's Island Recreation Area by walking across the footbridge over the Delaware River and turning right onto PA 32 north.
The Black Bass Inn is on the left as you leave the bridge on the Pennsylvania side of the river. The Delaware Canal State Park is located here between PA 32 and the Delaware River. This trail continues for 60 miles along the river and is a designated National Historic Landmark.

0.3 Turn left onto Fleecy Dale Road.
This sun-dappled road lined with wonderful old stone homes is one of the most scenic roads that our groups cycle on. There is another opportunity at the end of the tour to glide on Fleecy Dale Road.

2.4 Bear right across the stone bridge in Carversville onto Carversville Road.

2.5 Turn right immediately onto Wismer Road/Pipersville Road (which becomes Carversville-Wismer Road).
There is a steep uphill climb at the right turn onto Wismer Road.

7.0 Go through the covered bridge.
Be careful on the short, steep descent just before bridge. Because there are wooden floorboards on the bridge, it's safest to dismount and walk your bike here.

7.5 Turn left onto unmarked Dark Hollow Road.

7.8 Go straight onto PA 413 north/Old Easton Road.

8.0 Bear left onto Old Easton Road.

9.2 Cross PA 611 onto Saw Mill Road.
Be especially careful of the fast-moving traffic on this crossroad.

9.4 Turn left at the end of Saw Mill Road onto unmarked Scott Road.

12.4 Turn right at the end of Scott Road onto Smith School Road.

12.9 Turn left at the end of Smith School Road onto Deep Run Road (which becomes Hughes Lane).

13.4 Turn left at the end of Hughes Road onto Elephant Road.

13.6 At the traffic light in Dublin, go straight across PA 313 onto Maple Avenue. *You can stop for lunch at the Dublin IGA supermarket, which is about 0.4 mile to the right on PA 313. The supermarket has a bathroom. Then, return to the trafic light. Turn right to continue.*

Bear left immediately onto unmarked Middle Road.

14.9 Continue on Middle Road, passing Bypass Road.

15.7 Turn right at the end of Middle Road onto Upper Stump Road.

16.6 Turn left onto Upper Church Road.

17.1 Turn right at the end of Upper Church Road onto New Galena Road.

17.5 Turn left toward Sailor's Point on Lake Galena. *Lake Galena has picnic tables and bathrooms.*

Leave Lake Galena by going straight onto Myers Road. *There's a steep uphill just as you leave the lake.*

18.3 Merge straight onto Callowhill Road.

18.5 Turn right onto Upper Stump Road.

18.9 Turn left onto Upper Church Road.

20.2 Turn right onto unmarked Hilltown Pike.

20.4 Take the first right onto Dublin Road. *The Pearl S. Buck Home is on the left, just before the right onto Bypass Road.*

21.3 Take the first right after the Pearl S. Buck Home onto unmarked Bypass Road.

22.0 Turn left onto unmarked Middle Road.

23.3 Bear right onto Maple Avenue.

Cross PA 313 onto Elephant Road at the traffic light.

23.4 Take the first right onto Deep Run Road. *The ride becomes quite gentle, with pastoral views of the countryside toward the Delaware River.*

24.3 Turn left onto Twin Oaks Road.

24.6 Turn right onto Stony Bridge Road.

25.8 Go straight at the stop sign onto unmarked Deep Run Road.

26.6 Bear right at Irish Meetinghouse Road to continue on Deep Run Road.

27.9 Bear right onto Quarry Road.

Turn left immediately onto Deep Run Road.

28.6 Go straight across PA 611/Easton Road onto PA 413.

28.9 Turn left at the sign for PA 413.

29.3 Go straight across PA 413 onto Dark Hollow Road.

30.4 Make a hard right turn onto Covered Bridge Road as Dark Hollow Road veers to the left.
This turn is easy to miss. There are bathrooms on the right here.

31.0 Cross the covered bridge.
Walk your bike through the bridge; there are wooden floorboards on the bridge. There's a short, steep uphill just past the bridge.

31.3 Turn left to continue on Covered Bridge Road.

31.9 Go straight onto Tohickon Hill Road.

32.2 Turn right onto Tollgate Road.

32.7 Turn right onto Groveland Road.

33.6 Turn left onto Carversville-Wismer Road.
There's a very steep, winding downhill at the end of Carversville-Wismer Road.

36.2 Turn left at the end of Carversville-Wismer Road onto Carversville Road.

36.3 Turn left immediately in Carversville and bear right onto Fleecy Dale Road.

38.3 Turn right onto PA 32.

38.6 Turn left onto the footbridge over the Delaware River, returning to the Bull's Island Recreation Area.

Let Backcountry Guides Take You There

Our experienced backcountry authors will lead you to the finest trails, parks, and back roads in the following areas:

50 Hikes Series
50 Hikes in the Adirondacks
50 Hikes in Colorado
50 Hikes in Connecticut
50 Hikes in Central Florida
50 Hikes in North Florida
50 Hikes in South Florida
50 Hikes in the Lower Hudson Valley
50 Hikes in Kentucky
50 Hikes in the Maine Mountains
50 Hikes in Coastal and Southern Maine
50 Hikes in Louisiana
50 Hikes in Massachusetts
50 Hikes in Maryland
50 Hikes in Michigan
50 Hikes in the White Mountains
50 More Hikes in New Hampshire
50 Hikes in New Jersey
50 Hikes in Central New York
50 Hikes in Western New York
50 Hikes in the Mountains of North Carolina
50 Hikes in Ohio
50 More Hikes in Ohio
50 Hikes in Eastern Pennsylvania
50 Hikes in Central Pennsylvania
50 Hikes in Western Pennsylvania
50 Hikes in the Tennessee Mountains
50 Hikes in Vermont
50 Hikes in Northern Virginia
50 Hikes in Southern Virginia
50 Hikes in Wisconsin

Walking
Hikes & Walks in the Berkshire Hills
Walks and Rambles on Cape Cod and the Islands
Walks and Rambles on the Delmarva Peninsula
Walks and Rambles in the Western Hudson Valley
Walks and Rambles on Long Island
Walks and Rambles in Ohio's Western Reserve
Walks and Rambles in Rhode Island
Walks and Rambles in and around St. Louis
Weekend Walks in St. Louis and Beyond
Weekend Walks Along the New England Coast
Weekend Walks in Historic New England
Weekend Walks in the Historic Washington D.C. Region

Bicycling
25 Bicycle Tours in the Adirondacks
25 Bicycle Tours on Delmarva
25 Bicycle Tours in Savannah and the Carolina Low Country
25 Bicycle Tours in Maine
25 Bicycle Tours in Maryland
25 Bicycle Tours in the Twin Cities and Southeastern Minnesota
30 Bicycle Tours in New Jersey
25 Bicycle Tours in the Hudson Valley
25 Bicycle Tours in the Lake Champlain Region
25 Bicycle Tours in Maryland
25 Bicycle Tours in Ohio's Western Reserve
25 Bicycle Tours in the Texas Hill Country and West Texas
25 Bicycle Tours in Vermont
25 Bicycle Tours in and around Washington, D.C.
25 Mountain Bike Tours in the Adirondacks
25 Mountain Bike Tours in the Hudson Valley
25 Mountain Bike Tours in Massachusetts
25 Mountain Bike Tours in New Jersey
Backroad Bicycling in the Blue Ridge and Smoky Mountains
Backroad Bicycling in Connecticut
Backroad Bicycling on Cape Cod, Martha's Vineyard, and Nantucket
Backroad Bicycling in the Finger Lakes Region
Backroad Bicycling in Western Massachusetts
Backroad Bicycling in New Hampshire
Backroad Bicycling in Eastern Pennsylvania
Backroad Bicycling in Wisconsin
The Mountain Biker's Guide to Ski Resorts
Bicycling America's National Parks: Arizona & New Mexico
Bicycling America's National Parks: California
Bicycling America's National Parks: Oregon & Washington
Bicycling America's National Parks: Utah & Colorado
Bicycling Cuba

We offer many more books on hiking, fly-fishing, travel, nature, and other subjects. Our books are available at bookstores and outdoor stores everywhere. For more information or a free catalog, please call 1-800-245-4151 or write to us at The Countryman Press, P.O. Box 748, Woodstock, Vermont 05091. You can find us online at www.countrymapress.com.